Welcome to
iPhone
The Complete Manual

The iPhone is the complete mobile device. From making calls and taking pictures to browsing the web and listening to music, this incredible smartphone covers so many areas of your life you'll wonder how you'd ever live without it. In this book, we take you through every step of using your iPhone, including setting your device up, the common gestures you'll need to know, and the apps that open up a whole world of possibilities. The iPhone Complete Manual really is the best way to discover everything your iPhone has to offer. We hope you enjoy the book.

iPhone
The Complete Manual

Imagine Publishing Ltd
Richmond House
33 Richmond Hill
Bournemouth
Dorset BH2 6EZ
☎ +44 (0) 1202 586200
Website: www.imagine-publishing.co.uk
Twitter: @Books_Imagine
Facebook: www.facebook.com/ImagineBookazines

Head of Publishing
Aaron Asadi

Head of Design
Ross Andrews

Editor
Jon White

Senior Art Editor
William Shum

Design
Alison Innes

Photographer
James Sheppard

Printed by
William Gibbons, 26 Planetary Road, Willenhall, West Midlands, WV13 3XT

Distributed in the UK & Eire by
Imagine Publishing Ltd, www.imagineshop.co.uk. Tel 01202 586200

Distributed in Australia by
Gordon & Gotch, Equinox Centre, 18 Rodborough Road, Frenchs Forest,
NSW 2086. Tel + 61 2 9972 8800

Distributed in the Rest of the World by
Marketforce, Blue Fin Building, 110 Southwark Street, London, SE1 0SU

Part of the

iCreate
bookazine series

IMAGINE
PUBLISHING

Contents
What you can find inside the bookazine

Find out how to purchase and download all kinds of apps from the App Store on page 52

Suitable for all iPhones

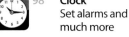

An introduction to iPhone

What makes the iPhone one of the best smartphones available? It's time to find out…

The original iPhone completely transformed the smartphone market. Its beautiful screen, versatility and fantastic built-in apps struck a chord with consumers and critics alike. It is built to run iOS, the operating system also used in the equally as impressive iPad and iPod touch, and so the general performance is as smooth as you could wish for. With finger-friendly icons and an environment that lets you get on with what you want to do, ease of use is apparent in every part of the software.

When you also consider the long battery life, exceptional build quality and near perfect screen, you start to realise that this is a smartphone built for anyone who wants to work and play anywhere. Thousands of apps are available to extend the experience as well and help you to get as much use as possible from one of the best phones money can buy.

No Service | 16:19
Mailboxes | Edit

📥 **Inbox**

⭐ **VIP**

📄 **Drafts**

📤 **Sent**

🗑 **Junk**

iCloud

The Mail app is able
to let you preview Office
documents when they are received

Fig 1 The simplistic Calendar app interface actually works well for complex agenda management

Get organised

The iPhone is packed full of useful functionality out of the box and the tools to get yourself organised are all included. First up is the Calendar app, which looks quite basic at first glance, but when you dig below the surface you start to realise that the simplistic interface is actually very useful when handling complex calendars (Fig 1). You can deal with more than one calendar at once and also accept invitations automatically.

The Reminders app lets you quickly add tasks that need to be done at a certain time and alerts will sound when required. You can even set Reminders to activate when you reach a particular location. The Clock app will wake you up with an alarm every day and also includes timers that can be used for time-dependent tasks (Fig 2). We shouldn't forget the Contacts app which will help you to detail every person you need and to add lots of information for each one.

Get work done

The iPhone is not just designed for fun and games; it can be utilised for work as well. The Mail app is able to let you preview Office documents when they are received and you can also use the well

Fig 2 The Clock app can deal with alarms, world times and instant timings

The inclusion of iTunes takes
your entertainment options
to a whole new level

thought-out keyboard for writing things down using the Notes app.
You can also utilise the Maps app to help you get to meetings and
to plan ahead so that you understand how much travelling time
you can expect.

As time has passed, the potential of the iPhone in the workplace
has been realised and there are thousands of apps available to
let you undertake specific tasks. However, for the basics and the
general day-to-day work tasks that take up most of your time, the
iPhone is able, from a software and hardware perspective, to help
you get everything done that you need to.

Enjoy yourself
The iPhone is perfect for keeping yourself and your family
entertained anywhere. The Videos app (Fig 3) lets you watch
movies for hours at a time before a charge is needed, perfect for
long distance flights, and the music quality is superb through
headphones and even the external speaker. The inclusion of iTunes
(Fig 4) takes your entertainment options to a whole new level. From
music to movies and from TV shows to iBooks, everything you
need is available to purchase and download straight to the iPhone

Fig 3 The battery allows hours of great
quality video playback. Perfect for those
long flights

Fig 4 Music, films, audiobooks, TV shows
– they are all available to buy through the
iTunes app

How the iPhone can improve your life

Productivity
The iWork suite of apps let you produce spreadsheets, presentations and documents easily and the touch interface makes work fun.

Lifestyle
Whether you want to improve your photos, make beautiful music or create home videos, you can do it all in style on an iPhone using the iLife suite of apps.

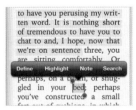

Entertainment
The free iBooks reader lets you purchase and read eBooks that look like paper titles and you can also watch full-screen videos and play music whenever you want to.

There are situations where the iPhone is perfect for providing entertainment

without the need for a PC. You can also create your own keepsakes using the camera or by transferring a photo collection to the iPhone for viewing whenever you want to remember a good time. There are many situations where the iPhone is perfect for providing entertainment and whether you want to simply read a book in bed or keep the kids amused on holiday, it is a great tool for keeping everyone happy.

Keep in touch
The iPhone is able to let you connect, in a variety of ways, to those who are important to you. FaceTime lets you speak to friends and family thousands of miles away and the quality of the video stream

iPhone accessories

Lightning to 30-pin Adaptor
This adaptor will let you connect a huge range of accessories designed for previous generation iPhones to the latest versions, which will open up the number of accessories you can use.

Headphones
If you're looking to enjoy media on the move, it's worth investing in a quality pair of headphones. This will also ensure you don't annoy other people when on your commute!

Camera lens
If you like taking pictures, then the iPhone's incredible camera will be one of the major selling points. Take things further by purchasing a clip-on lens, allowing you to zoom, apply effects and more.

Speakers
Your iPhone can act as the perfect music device, and part of this is sharing music with friends. A good speaker can help you be the life and soul of the party.

Battery pack
If you're a heavy user, you may find that your iPhone's regularly running out of battery power. Investing in a battery pack will give your iPhone an extra boost when it most needs it.

Wireless storage
There are a number of devices you can purchase that will allow you to upload files and images onto a portable device, freeing up space on your phone. You can also transfer data and stream media from your phone.

The music quality
is superb through
headphones and
the speaker

Fig 5 Siri enables you to give instructions vocally and hear the results without any typing at all

brings everything to life. Messages works like standard instant messaging, but it is completely free and will work across multiple devices, including Macs and iPads, so that you can keep the conversation going all of the time.

Of course there is a capable email app included and the ability to access multiple social networks via the Safari app or through third-party solutions is also open to you. iPhone users can also enjoy asking their devices questions and assigning it tasks, such as sending messages, using the Siri service (Fig 5). So you can even use your iPhone to connect with other people using only the power of your voice – now that's progress.

Top iPhone applications

Facebook
Stay in touch effortlessly with this app that is even integrated into the iOS to allow you to post from other apps.

Sky+
A must if you are a Sky+ subscriber as it allows you to browse TV listings and set your box to record remotely.

Instagram
A cool social network for photo fans. Take pics through this app and apply all manner of special FX on the fly.

Podcasts
Search through hundreds of different podcasts, subscribe and then listen to them through this handy app.

AmpliTube
Plug in your electric guitar using the iRig adaptor and enjoy a range of great-sounding amps and effects.

Temple Run 2
A great-looking, fast-paced action game with a dynamic control system that will test your reflexes to the limit.

BBC iPlayer
Ensure that you never miss your favourite BBC programmes with this essential portable viewing portal.

eBay
Browse, watch and track your purchases on the move with this handy mobile shopping app.

YouTube
Since the release of iOS 6 this is available as a free download as is a rich source of visual entertainment.

You can even use your iPhone to connect with other people using only the power of your voice – now that's progress

Set up your iPhone

We show you how to activate your iPhone for the first time and familiarise yourself with this wondrous device

1 **Turn your iPhone on** To turn on your iPhone for the first time, press and hold the On/Off button (the lozenge-shaped button on the top right of the tablet) for about three seconds. If your iPhone is new or has been recently reset you should be greeted with the Apple logo and then, after ten seconds or so, a plain screen with 'iPhone' written on it (Fig 1).

2 **Resetting a pre-owned iPhone** If, when you turn your iPhone on via the On/Off button, you are taken straight to the Home Screen, then your iPhone is already activated. If you wish to reset the iPhone so you can set it up as new, go to the Settings app and scroll down to the Reset option and Erase All Contents And Settings. You can then follow this tutorial to activate your iPhone as new.

Fig 1, Turn on **Fire up your iPhone**

3 **Slide to unlock** At the plain-looking iPhone screen (as shown in Fig 1), you need to slide your finger to the right across the arrow at the bottom of the screen to continue. At this screen the iPhone is locked (as shown by the padlock icon in the top-centre of the screen). You will need to perform the sliding motion every time you wish to wake the iPhone up, so get used to it!

4 **Waking up the iPhone** If at any point during the activation process the iPhone goes to 'sleep' (the screen goes blank), usually because it was left unattended, you can wake it up simply by pressing the Home button (the circular one at the bottom-centre of the iPhone's front) or tapping the On/Off button (don't hold it). You'll then have to unlock your iPhone as shown in Step 3.

5 **Select your language** Once you've unlocked your iPhone, you will see a short list of common languages to choose from. If the language that you'd like is not in this list, tap the downwards arrow. You will then be presented with a list of different languages (Fig 2). The language you choose here will be the language that your device is set to. Tap the blue and white arrow in the top-right corner.

Fig 2, Select language **Choose from the list**

6 **Select your Country or Region** Now, similar to choosing your language, you will have a short list of countries/regions to choose from (Fig 3). If your country or region is not in the list, tap 'Show More...' and pick yours from there. This will determine the apps that are available in the App Store and the various media available from the iTunes app, as well as the correct currency.

Slide your finger along the slider at the bottom of the screen to unlock your iPhone

Fig 3, Select your region **This affects apps**

Introducing iPhone

Set up your iPhone

Fig 4, Location Services **This is used by apps**

Fig 5, Connect to Wi-Fi **Scan for networks**

Fig 6, Set Up iPhone **Choose an option**

7 **Location Services** The next part of the process is dedicated to your device's Location Services (Fig 4). This allows apps to gather and use data indicating your approximate location, which is incredibly useful if you ever lose your device. For a more detailed explanation on the service, tap 'What is Location Services?' towards the bottom of the screen. Tap 'Done' when you've finished.

8 **Enable or Disable** You must either enable or disable the Location Services service by tapping on your chosen option – there is no option to skip the step. If you are still unsure of the purpose of this feature and need more information then don't worry; you can activate it later from the Settings app in the Home Screen. Tap 'Next' to continue the activation process.

9 **Connect to a Wi-Fi network** Your iPhone will be able to connect to the internet wirelessly via a Wi-Fi connection. If you have a Wi-Fi network set up in your house it will appear in the menu (Fig 5). Tap on it and you will need to enter your password using the on-screen keyboard. When you've entered the password, tap the Join button either on the keyboard or the dialog box.

10 **If you don't have a Wi-Fi connection…** If you can't access a Wi-Fi connection, but you do have a computer with iTunes installed, you can continue the activation by connecting your iPhone to the computer via the supplied USB cable and then choosing the 'Connect to iTunes' option beneath any other wireless networks the iPhone could pick up.

11 **Set Up iPhone** The next screen you'll see will present you with three options: Set Up as New iPhone, Restore from iCloud Backup, and Restore from iTunes Backup (Fig 6). You will most likely want to choose the first option, which requires no more than a tap of the 'Next' button in the top right to continue with the activation (Step 14). However, we will also look at the other choices…

12 **Restore from iCloud Backup** You should choose this option if you have an iCloud account that has a backup attached to it. Once you've chosen and tapped 'Next' you'll have to enter the Apple ID of the account that has the backup, and its password. You'll then be able to restore the iPhone from the backup. New iPhone owners won't use this.

You can also activate your iPhone via iTunes by connecting it to a computer via USB

13 **Restore from iTunes Backup** If you choose this option you can restore your iPhone from a backup kept on your desktop computer in iTunes. Connect your iPhone to your computer via the USB cable and select the backup you want to use from iTunes. Note that you can also set the iPhone as a new one (as if you tapped the 'Set Up as New iPhone' button in Step 11) from here.

14 **Apple ID** The Apple ID, which you create in the next step of the activation, is one of the most important things you will do during the process. A tap of the 'What is an Apple ID?' link at the bottom of the screen tells you why ownership of an Apple ID is essential. You will need one to download apps from the App Store, buy songs from iTunes and purchase books from iBooks.

15 **Create an Apple ID** If you have yet to create an Apple ID, it's incredibly simple to do so, and you do can do it from the comfort of your iPhone. Tap the Create a Free Apple ID button (Fig 7) and you'll have to enter your birthday (which will be used in case you forget your password), your name, and the email address that will eventually become your Apple ID.

Fig 7 , Apple ID **You need one of these**

16 **Sign In with an Apple ID** Due to the exceptional success of Apple programs like iTunes, you may already have an Apple ID without so much as touching an iPhone, Mac, iPhone, or iPod. If you have one, tap Sign In with an Apple ID and enter your ID and password. If you know you own one but can't remember the details, tap 'Forgot Apple ID or Password?' and you'll be able to retrieve it.

17 **Read the Terms & Conditions** After signing in with either your brand new or existing Apple ID, you will be presented with a screen of Terms and Conditions that relate to all aspects of your iPhone and the services that you will be using, such as iCloud, Game Center and so on. If you wish to read them on a larger screen, you can email them to yourself by tapping the 'Send by Email' button.

Fig 8, T&Cs **You must agree to these**

18 **All about iCloud** After 30 seconds or so, you will have the opportunity to set up one of the most revolutionary services Apple has created: iCloud – a fantastic cloud service that enable you to wirelessly keep your contacts, emails and calendars across multiple devices without you having to do anything. Tap 'What is iCloud' (Fig 9) to find out more about how it can benefit your life.

An Apple ID enables you to buy music, movies and books straight from the comfort of your iPhone

Fig 9, iCloud **There to make your life easier**

Set up your iPhone

Fig 10, Find My iPhone **Locate a lost device**

Fig 11, Complete! **Start using your iPhone**

Fig 12, Home screen **Have fun!**

19 **Enable or disable iCloud** Tap the top option to enable iCloud – it's free (although there is the option to pay to increase your storage space, which you can do in Settings). If you choose not to enable it, you will miss the opportunity to set up Find My iPhone in the next step of the process. You can, however, enable it from the Settings app once you've completed the activation.

20 **The Find My iPhone service** If you misplace your iPhone then Find My iPhone will help you locate it on a map, play a sound or display a message. You can activate this service to sync the location of your device with your iCloud (Fig 10). If you lose your iPhone then you can access the service from an iPhone, iPod touch or computer by visiting **www.icloud.com**.

21 **Diagnostics and Usage** The next screen deals with diagnostics and usage data. Basically, Apple likes to keep track of how its products are performing, so this screen allows you to send diagnostic data straight to Apple. If you wish to keep your information private, opt for 'Don't Send'. You can change your answer after activation from the Settings app, in the 'About' tab.

22 **Your last chance to restart** The diagnostics screen offers you one last chance to restart the activation process if you're not happy with the choices you've made. To restart the process, tap the Home button (the circular button at the bottom of the iPhone) once, and a menu should pop up. You will then find the option to restart the activation, where you can make the choices you want.

23 **Set up is complete!** Congratulations! You have now worked your way through the entire set-up process. A screen will confirm that the process is complete (Fig 11), so what are you waiting for? Tap on the 'Start Using iPhone' button to start using your iPhone! If you press the Home button now to restart the procedure, you will just be taken to the Home Screen instead.

24 **Start using your iPhone** You'll be presented with your Home screen (Fig 12), so start tapping on icons to launch apps and find your way around and experiment with the gestures needed to operate your new device. Tap the Settings app and you'll have access to countless options, including ones that can reset the choices you made during the activation process.

You can change most of the choices you made during activation in the Settings app

The iPhone Home screen

Time
You can change the format of the iPhone's clock in the Settings app

Battery
This little icon will tell you how much battery power you have left

Wi-Fi
This icon shows that you're connected to a network. See the icons below for more info

The apps
The heart and soul of the iPhone. Tap on an icon to launch the app

Wallpaper
Your iPhone's background is called the wallpaper. You can change it from the Settings app

The dock
Many people choose to place to their most-used apps here in the Dock

Common iPhone icons

 Wi-Fi
This icon shows that your iPhone is successfully connected to the internet via a Wi-Fi network

 3G
If you see this icon then you're connected to the web over a 3G network. Not all iPhones have this

 4G
If you have a newer iPhone, you may have access to the internet over 4G; in which case, this icon will be displayed

 Airplane mode
If you put your iPhone in Airplane mode then you can't access the internet or Bluetooth. Look for this icon

 Lock
This tells you that your iPhone is locked. Slide your finger across the bottom of the screen to unlock it

 Do Not Disturb
If your iPhone is set to Do Not Disturb mode then this icon will appear in the top-middle of the screen

 Battery
The icon in the top-right shows you how much power you have left. A lightning bolt will show it's charging

 Activity
The Activity icon will show up when something is happening on your iPhone. Continue using it as normal

 Screen orientation lock
If you've set your iPhone to stop switching from landscape to portrait, then you'll see this icon

 Alarm
Set an Alarm in the Clock app and this icon will appear in the top right, telling you that your Alarm is active

 Location Services
The Location Services icon will appear to tell you that your iPhone is determining your current location

 Bluetooth
If you're paired with another device via Bluetooth, then this icon will show in the top-right-corner of the screen

How to use your iPhone

Learn how you can navigate and control your smartphone

Using an iPhone is all about touch. There are very few hardware buttons included aside from the Home button on the front, the On/Off button at the top and the volume and mute keys on the side – so it's amazing that the iPhone is capable of doing so much. As well as the basic tasks that you would expect it do – turn on and off, go on standby, etc – you can use its incredible multi-touch screen in combination with the buttons to multitask and arrange and manage your apps to your heart's content. Here are some of the basic actions you need to know about when navigating your iPhone.

Turn your iPhone off and on

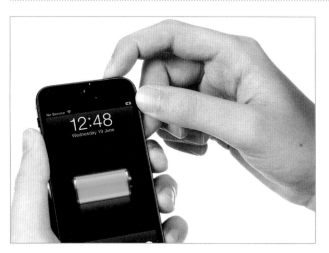

1 **The power button** Hold down the On/Off button (at the top of the iPhone) for a couple of seconds to turn the iPhone on from a cold start. The 'Slide to Unlock' screen will appear quite quickly.

2 **Turn off** Hold the On/Off button for a few seconds when the iPhone's on.

3 **Slide to turn off** Slide the red slider at the top to turn your iPhone off.

Put your iPhone to sleep

1 **Don't hold it** Press the On/Off button as normal, but do not hold it down for too long.

2 **Standby mode** The screen will go blank and the iPhone is now in standby mode ready to start again.

Charging your iPhone

1 Use the kit Plug the charger cable into the bottom of the iPhone.

2 Plug it Plug the cable into the AC adaptor that comes with the iPhone.

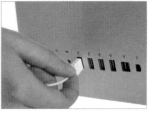

3 USB You can charge the iPhone by USB, but it's not the quickest.

Multitasking

2 Select apps Slide your finger along the strip and tap on an app to load it.

1 Double-tap Home No matter what app you are in or where you are, double-tap the Home button to bring up the multitasking strip at the bottom of the screen. You should see more icons.

3 Close it Tap and hold on an app, then tap the red 'X' to close it down.

Manage your apps

2 Tap and drag Tap and hold on an app and drag it around to move it.

1 The Home Screen To navigate the Home Screen you will mostly use the swipe gesture to switch between multiple screens of icons. Simply swipe to the left to see the next screen and the right to return to the first.

3 Folders Drag one app over another to create an app folder.

Change the volume with headphones

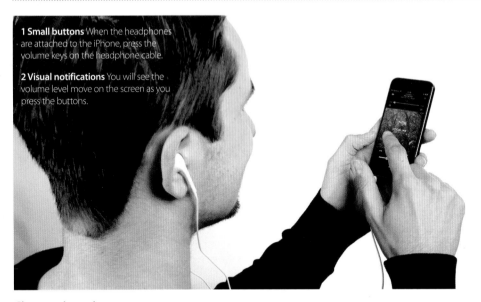

1 Small buttons When the headphones are attached to the iPhone, press the volume keys on the headphone cable.

2 Visual notifications You will see the volume level move on the screen as you press the buttons.

Change the volume

1 The standard way In any app or in the Home Screen, you can simply press the volume key up or down to adjust the volume to your preference. This is the quickest way to adjust the sound levels.

2 Via Multitasking Double-tap the Home button then swipe right.

3 Volume bar Now you can move the bar to your preferred volume.

Muting

2 Use the keys Hold the volume down button to mute.

1 The Mute button Slide the small button above the volume keys until you see a red marker. This will mute the iPhone immediately, which is useful if you need to quickly stop any alerts or unwanted sounds from being heard.

3 Multitasking In the multitasking bar, move the slider all the way left.

Set the rotation lock

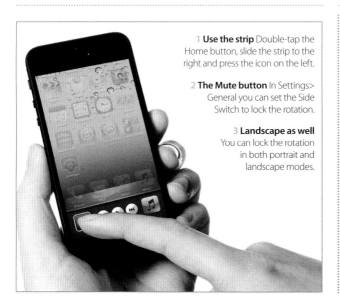

1 Use the strip Double-tap the Home button, slide the strip to the right and press the icon on the left.

2 The Mute button In Settings> General you can set the Side Switch to lock the rotation.

3 Landscape as well You can lock the rotation in both portrait and landscape modes.

Set the brightness

1 Open Settings Tap on the Settings icon and select Brightness & Wallpaper.

2 Slide for brightness Drag the slider left or right to increase and decrease the brightness.

Fig 1, Tap You will need to tap to launch apps

Fig 2, Scroll Drag your finger to navigate around

Fig 3, Swipe Use this gesture to switch pages

Fig 4, Drag Keep your finger held down

Fig 5, Pinch Use this gesture to zoom out

Hand gestures on your iPhone

Learn the many ways you can control your iPhone using the power of your fingers

1 **Tap** Tapping is the main way you will navigate your iPhone. To open an app, you must tap it from your Home Screen, for example (Fig 1). You'll mainly be tapping the iPhone to select things like web links in Safari, songs in Music, or pictures in Photos. You'll also need to tap to type on the on-screen keyboard when it appears in numerous apps such as Mail, Messages, Reminders and Notes.

2 **Scroll** Scrolling is when you drag your finger up or down the iPhone's screen (Fig 2). This is most useful when the iPhone can't fit all the information on one screen, so you need to slide your finger up to move the screen down and vice versa. This is most common in apps like Safari, Notes and, depending on the size of your collections, Music & Videos.

3 **Swipe** Where scrolling is vertical, swiping is horizontal – you just need to move your finger from left to right or vice versa. Once you start filling your iPhone up with apps, you'll need to swipe to switch between pages of apps on the Home Screen (Fig 3). It's also needed to flick through the pages of your ebooks in iBooks and your magazines in Newsstand.

4 **Drag** Dragging is when you tap and hold your finger on the iPhone, then drag it anywhere else on the screen. It's essential when moving apps around on the Home Screen. Tap and hold on an app until all other apps start wobbling. You can now drag it to its rightful place on the Home Screen. It's rarely used in other native apps, but common in third-party games.

5 **Pinch** Widely used among built-in and third-party apps, the pinch is a very useful gesture. To perform it, place two fingers on the screen and bring them together (Fig 5). It won't do anything on the Home Screen, but in many apps, including Photos and Maps, it zooms out the display. The more distance between your two fingers, the larger the zoom.

6 **Spread** The spread is essentially the opposite to the pinch: rather than bringing two digits together, you spread them apart (annotated image). The effect is also the opposite, as rather than zooming out, you zoom in instead. This is particularly useful in Safari, when perhaps you need to zoom in read particularly small text; or Photos, when you want to inspect an image close-up.

Spread
By spreading your fingers apart, you'll be able to zoom in on the screen. The feature is useful in apps such as Maps

Screen
With so much of the iPhone's features controlled via the screen, it's essential to master how best to use the touch-based controls

Tapping
Tapping on the screen is likely to be the most common gesture you use on your iPhone

Accessibility
If you're finding the gestures difficult to master, there are plenty of options in the Accessibility menu to make things easier

"Tapping is the main way you will navigate your iPhone"

Settings

✈	Airplane Mode	OFF
🛜	Wi-Fi	SKY42DDC >
❁	Bluetooth	Off >
🌐	Personal Hotspot	Off >

Fig 1, Settings Personalise your iPhone

Fig 2, App Store Home to over 750,000 apps

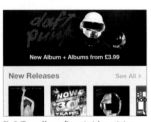

Fig 3, iTunes Your online entertainment store

Fig 4, Music It's easy to listen to tunes in Music

Fig 5, Safari Browsing with tabs in Safari

Applications

Your at-a-glance guide to what Apple's built-in iPhone apps and App Store products can do for you

 Settings This is where you'll be able to change how your iPhone works. You can connect to Wi-Fi, passcode-protect your device, and update the software, among many other things – all from this app. See page 32.

 Phone If you want to make calls on your iPhone then the Phone app allows you to access a keypad for inputting new numbers, browse your contacts database and much more. See page 44.

 Messages As well as sending normal text messages, you can also take advantage of iMessage – a free messaging service that enables you to text users with other iOS devices for free. See page 48.

 App Store Although the built-in apps on your iPhone are fantastic and will benefit your life in many different ways, you can download and buy more apps from Apple's built-in App Store. See page 52.

 iTunes Through this service you can download the hottest new albums and films, all from the comfort of your sofa. Just search for what you want, tap to buy and you'll have it in minutes. See page 58.

 Music Through this app you can listen to all of your purchased iTunes music, or music that you've transferred to your iPhone. You can also set up playlists, rate your music collection and more. See page 64.

 Videos All of the TV shows and movies that you've downloaded from iTunes, along with any that you've transferred from your computer, will be viewable through this simple but effective app. See page 68.

 Safari This app is the best way to browse the internet on your iPhone. Provided you're connected to Wi-Fi, you can use Safari to surf the web with tabs, browse privately or add items to read offline. See page 72.

 Mail Round-the-clock access to your email account is vital in today's world. The iPhone Mail app helps you achieve this with an easy setup process and an intuitive interface. See page 78.

 Calendar If you need to organise your life, then check out the this app. It enables you to set up events, schedule appointments and basically take control of your day, week, month or even year! See page 82.

 Reminders If you find yourself regularly forgetting to do various tasks, use the Reminders app to give you a nudge. Set priorities and the exact times at which you need to be reminded. See page 86.

Passbook This app allows you to download digital tickets – be it vouchers for discounted items, hotel reservations or plane tickets – and then present them for scanning from your iPhone's screen. See page 88.

Notes Whether you need to jot down something important or just a whimsical thought, the easy-to-use Notes has you covered. All of your notes can also be synced to iCloud. See page 90.

Maps This app will help you keep track of where you are in the world. It'll give you directions and show you how bad the traffic situation is, among many other things. See page 92.

FaceTime With your iPhone's high quality built-in cameras you can chat face-to-face with someone on another iOS device for free using a Wi-Fi connection. See page 100.

Camera It may surprise you, but your iPhone is capable of taking some very good pictures – especially the newer models. So use the exceptional built-in Camera app to your advantage. See page 104.

Photos Once you've taken your photos or videos, you'll need a place to view them. Luckily, the Photos app is the perfect place for you to marvel at your images, and even make edits to them. See page 108.

Game Center Take advantage of the millions of games available on iPhone with Game Center. The app tracks your achievements and has leaderboards for many of the top games on iPhone. See page 112.

Newsstand The iPhone has revolutionised digital media and its built-in Newsstand app is the best way to the consume it. Read digital magazines and newspapers with ease. See page 116.

iBooks If you fancy reading some a bit more traditional on your iPhone, then check out iBooks and the iBookstore. Here there are thousands of ebooks, which can all be read the way you want. See page 120.

Pages This app turns your iPhone into an amazing mobile word processor. You can create documents on the go in style by downloading Pages from the App Store. See page 124.

GarageBand By downloading this easy-to-master music-making app from the App Store, you can create multi-layered masterpieces with very little music knowledge. See page 134.

iMovie If you want to turn your iPhone movies into something special, then look no further. You can cut trailers, add special effects, and turn your family into the stars of professional-looking films. See page 136.

iPhoto While the Photos app enables you to make rudimentary edits to your images, iPhoto is packed full of effects, brushes and swatches to make your photos stand out from the pack. See page 140.

Fig 6, Reminders **Never forget anything again**

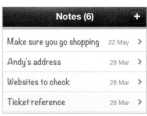

Fig 7, Notes **Jot down ideas and lists**

Fig 8, Maps **Use Maps to find your way**

Fig 9, Photos **Your virtual photo album**

Fig 10, Game Center **Challenge your friends**

Settings

Settings

We provide you with a guided tour around the nerve centre of your iPhone

You'll use it to…

Connect to the internet
Establish a Wi-Fi connection to your device

Manage notifications
Determine how your iPhone alerts you to various things

Personalise your iPhone
Change the wallpaper, accessibility of your device and much more

Manage your iCloud
Connect to your cloud, and manage your storage and backup

Enable restrictions
Passcode-protect your device and set age restrictions on apps

Get social
Log into your Twitter and Facebook accounts to integrate them into your apps

Fig 1 (above) In the Settings app, the functions and sections appear in a simple, staggered list

Fig 2 (right) Tap 'Edit' in your Notifications settings and press and hold on the list icon next to an app to change the order

Take control of your iPhone

The Settings app, which you can launch by tapping its icon on the Home screen, is where you can tailor the functionality of your iPhone to suit your needs, as well as personalise its appearance and services. In Settings, the categories are laid out in a list, broken down into key sections as you scroll down the page (Fig 1).

Notification Center

Your iPhone is constantly alerting you to new things – incoming emails, messages, Game Center friend requests and other assorted app alerts – and Notification Center lets you keep track of them easily by accessing a handy drop-down panel. To access your Notification Center, you swipe down from the top of the screen and all of your recent notifications will be displayed in a list. To tailor your Notification Center to your own specific needs, launch the Settings app and then tap on the Notifications section from the main Settings list. The main screen presents a list of apps that are in your Notification Center (and a list of those that are not, which you can add to the list). By tapping the Edit button in

the top-right corner you can move apps between lists and change the order of how the apps appear in your Notification Center (Fig 2). To determine how your iPhone receives alerts, tap on an app in the list and you can set the style of alert (how and where it will appear) and also whether or not it will flash up on your Lock screen.

Connect to the internet via Wi-Fi

iCloud

Apple's iCloud service is free to use and stores your music, photos, documents and more, and wirelessly sends them to all of your iOS devices (and Macs running OS X Mountain Lion) without you having to manually transfer files. Many of the built-in iPhone apps, such as Contacts, Calendars and Reminders, use iCloud in some form to sync data across devices. You can determine which apps use iCloud by launching your Settings app and tapping iCloud. Move the sliders of the apps you wish to benefit from iCloud to the On position.

Manage your iCloud storage

Your iCloud account comes with five gigabytes of free storage as standard. To check how much space you have, tap on the Storage & Backup option in the iCloud section of Settings. To see how much of your free storage your apps use, tap on the Manage Storage option. You can delete data by tapping on an app and selecting the Edit button in the top-right corner. If you wish to buy more storage space for your iCloud, tap on the Buy More Storage option and then choose a capacity and price plan that suits you from the list. While iCloud will automatically back-up your data if you have the iCloud Backup slider option turned on, you can also do this manually whenever you wish by tapping the Back Up Now option.

1 Go to Wi-Fi Settings
In Settings, tap on Wi-Fi and ensure that the slider is turned on.

2 Choose network
Your device will scan for networks. Tap on a Wi-Fi network to select it.

3 Enter password
You'll be prompted to enter your password. Do so, then tap 'Join'.

4 Connected
A tick will indicate that you are connected to your network.

You can view your personal iCloud account information by tapping on the account name

33

Settings

Wirelessly update your iPhone

Before October 2011, you had to connect your iPhone to a computer and then use the iTunes app to update your system's software. Now times have changed and a computer is no longer required. You can activate and set up your iPhone completely wirelessly and download free software updates on your device – as long as you have a Wi-Fi connection (see page 33 for how to connect your iPhone to the internet). If you don't, you'll still have to connect to iTunes.

If your iPhone's operating system (iOS) is out of date and there is a new, free update available then you will be notified via a small red alert that appears next to your Settings app icon. When this occurs, launch your Settings app and then tap on the General section in the

Software update
The '1' in the General section means you have a Software Update available. Tap 'General' then 'Software Update'

Available storage
Tap on the Storage & Backup option under the iCloud section to review how much storage space you have left

Notifications
All of the aspects of how your iPhone alerts you can be found here, from which apps send you notifications, to the manner in which they do

Your iCloud account
Your iCloud account is tied in with your iTunes account that you have set up on your device to purchase media and apps

You can back up your
iPhone to iCloud straight
away by tapping on the
'Back Up Now' option

settings list. At the top of this page will be an option called Software
Update (Fig 3) – tap on this and your device will start scanning for
new updates, provided it is connected to a Wi-Fi network. If a new
update is detected then you can opt to download and install it on
your device. Be warned though that this may take a few minutes
and your device will restart when the process is complete.

Back up your iPhone

As you will have all sorts of important stuff on your iPhone, iCloud
will provide peace of mind by automatically backing up your device
daily over Wi-Fi when your device is connected to a power source.
Once you plug it in, everything is backed up without you having
to lift a finger. When you set up a new iPhone or need to restore
the information on one you already have, iCloud does all the heavy
lifting for you. Just connect your device to Wi-Fi, enter your Apple
ID (which you created when you activated your iPhone), and then
all your purchased music, TV shows, books and apps, will appear on
your device. To activate this service, launch your Settings app and
tap on the iCloud section. Next, tap on the Storage & Backup option
and ensure iCloud Backup is turned on.

How to back up your iPhone

1 Go to iCloud Settings
Tap on the Storage & Backup option
and turn on the iCloud Backup option.

2 Initiate back up
Ensure that your iPhone is plugged in,
locked and connected to Wi-Fi.

Set keyboard shortcuts

1 Access keyboard settings
In the Settings app, tap on
General and then Keyboard.

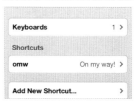

2 Enable shortcuts
Move the shortcut sliders to 'On'
to enable the various features.

3 Adding shortcuts
Tap on Add New Shortcut to start
adding your own.

4 Creating shortcuts
Type in a word or phrase followed
by the shortcut you wish to use.

35

Set a passcode

1 Tap Passcode Lock
In the General section in Settings, tap on the Passcode Lock options.

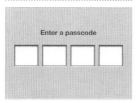

2 Turn it on
Tap on the Turn Passcode On option at the top of the page.

3 Enter a code
Enter and confirm a four-digit code to protect your device.

4 Secure passcode
Turn off Simple Passcode to use your full keyboard for a code.

To prevent other users buying apps, change the Require Password option to 'Immediately'

Change the Wallpaper
If you want to change the appearance of your iPhone then you can do so under the Brightness and Wallpaper settings. When you tap on this option you will see the brightness options at the top – which basically consists of a slider to adjust the brightness and an option to activate Auto-Brightness.

To change the wallpaper, tap on the Wallpaper options and you will be presented with two sections to tap on. The first, called Wallpaper, allows you to choose from a selection of pre-loaded wallpapers that are already installed on your device and the second, called Camera Roll, lets you fashion a background out of a photograph in your Photos app. Whichever option you choose, tap on your selection and it will be displayed full-screen. Now simply tap either the Set Lock Screen or Set Home Screen buttons to instantly set the image as your chosen backdrop on either your Lock Screen or your Home Screen. Alternatively, tap on the Set Both option to use the same image for both screens.

There are many apps available from the App Store that provide hundreds of great additional wallpapers for your device. These can be downloaded to your Photos app and then used from there.

Impose restrictions

1 Tap on Restrictions
In the General Settings page, tap on the Restrictions section.

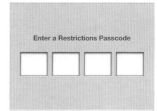

2 Enable restrictions
Tap on Enable Restrictions and then set a four-digit passcode.

Enable parental restrictions

As you have invested quite a significant sum of money in your iPhone, as well as the various apps and iTunes media content that you have bought, then you will naturally want to impose restrictions on who can access your material. Likewise, if your device is shared throughout the family then enabling restrictions will mean that inappropriate material cannot be accessed through the device and expensive apps can't be purchased by accident.

To start enabling restrictions, go to the General Settings section and then tap on Restrictions. By tapping on the Enable Restrictions option at the top of the page, you will first be required to enter a four-digit passcode. Do so and then move the sliders to the On position of the apps that may be accessed and then review the list of allowed content (Fig 4). To impose greater restrictions, go back to the General page and tap on Passcode Lock (Fig 5).

Fig 4 Use the sliders in this list to completely customise and tailor the restrictions on your iPhone, preventing accidental purchases

Restrictions
If your device is used regularly by others, then you can set certain restrictions to protect your device, and them, from tapping on the wrong thing

Auto-Lock
Activate this feature to decide on the time period before you iPhone goes to sleep and locks itself after inactivity on your part

Passcode lock
If you wish to stop people getting easy access to your device, why not set up a passcode lock?

Keyboard
You can set the keyboard up to be both easier to use and quicker to type by adjusting the various Keyboard settings

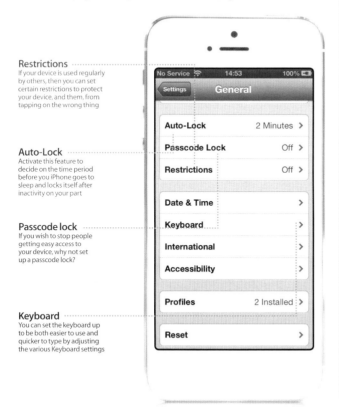

Fig 5 To impose greater restrictions and gain more control over what your kids can do, turn on the Passcode Lock function

Set the date & time

1 Go to Settings
Launch your Settings app and scroll down and tap General.

2 Tap on Date & Time
When you see the Date & Time option, tap on it to open.

3 Turn off automatic
Disable the Set Automatically slider and tap on Set Date & Time.

4 Set details
You can now manually set the date and time on your device.

To access the Spotlight search, swipe with one finger from left to right on the Home screen

Customise and access Spotlight

As if finding things on your iPhone wasn't simple enough, the built-in Spotlight Search function lets you type criteria into a search field and then unearth it instantly. To use this feature, simply swipe right from your device's primary Home Screen and then the screen will dim, a small search field will appear and your iPhone's keyboard will pop up to allow you to enter keywords into the search field. The results will appear below.

In Settings, you can determine what is searched for and the order in which the results appear. To check this out for yourself, go to the General section in Settings and you should see a category called 'Spotlight Search'. Tap on this. The screen that you are taken to is little more than a list of search categories that relate to content on your device. You can activate or deactivate content to search for in this list and the order of the items reflects the order in which the search results will be displayed.

To change the order in which the search results are displayed, press and hold on the list icon next to each category and then drag it up or down into a new position and then release so that it snaps into place – that's all there is to it.

How to tweak Accessibility

1 Scroll Through Settings
Within the Settings app, scroll down to General, tap, then select Accessibility.

2 iPhone for All
This section is filled with extra visual and hearing aids to help users.

Improving your iPhone's Accessibility

The iPhone may be designed to look and feel like a high-end and luxury product, but the beauty of it is that it is accessible to and for everyone. The Accessibility settings are the perfect example of the iPhone's user friendliness regardless of age, tech experience or health impairments. In this section of your Settings you will find tools to increase the text size. Simply tap the Large Text option and then select your preferred font size from the list that appears. There is also a slider to invert the colours on your screen – a very handy tool if you're colour blind (Fig 6). Create extra or easier shortcuts for yourself and use the Speak Auto-text slider option to turn on/off voice notifications of any changes made to the things you type on your iPhone. Suddenly this cutting-edge piece of technology isn't so daunting.

Fig 6 Inverting colours may help if you happen to be colour blind

Guided Access
Place a single, additional app on your Home Screen from which users can access the key feature of their iPhone

Home-click Speed
Alter the speed with which you have to double click the Home button in order to return to the Home Screen

Incoming Calls
Tweak the route you receive incoming calls through if you're using a headset or speaker with your iPhone

Triple-click Home
Turn on this additional shortcut and choose an essential function to be performed upon a triple click

Contacts

With the Contacts app, you can access and edit
your contact lists from personal, business and
organisational accounts

You'll use it to...

Access Contacts
Maintain personal and business details

Edit Contacts
Add and delete details

Search Contacts
Access your contacts quickly

Address emails quickly
Open an email from the Contacts section

Sync contacts
Transfer Contacts to multiple devices

Assign photos
Attach a photo to a contact for visual
recognition of a person

Fig 1 (above) Use the Contacts information
within other apps, adding efficiency
and convenience

Fig 2 (right) To enter data on each template
line, touch the line and enter data via the
iPhone's floating keyboard

Manage your contacts

Contacts allow you to not only access your friends and associates
but you can edit them from a selection of personal and business
accounts. You can also search for details within thanks to a easy
search field and send emails by clicking on an address (Fig 1).

Add, edit and delete Contacts

To add a contact on the iPhone you need to tap the Contacts
app, which will open the Contacts window. This displays a list of
contacts, in alphabetical
order, on the the screen with
letter-by-letter shortcuts on
the right hand side.

To Edit your contact
database and add a new
contact, tap the '+' button
situated in the top right
corner of the screen. A
new screen will open
up displaying an empty
template which you can fill
in via the pop-up keyboard
present at the base of the
screen (Fig 2). When you
have completed the page,
press Done to close the
record and return to the
index. To edit an existing
record, press the Edit button
situated in the top right
of the screen when on a

contact's information page. This time, the completed template will
be present with options to either change the text or delete entire
lines of information using the swivelling red buttons that turn into
delete buttons when touched.

Add extra information to your contacts

When you access the edit screen for
a contact, you are presented with a
standard template array that asks you basic
information. You can, however, add further
information if you wish which is not readily
observable from the basic edit page. To see it,
you have to press the '+' key next to the add
field box, which can be found at the bottom
of the edit page. This will bring a new
window displaying a wide choice of extra fields, including Twitter
and Facebook information, nickname, Instant Message information,
birthday and related people. You can even add notes should you
want to get really specific with how you know them. You really can
cover every aspect of every person you know.

Contacts & iCloud

Keep your contact details, including your mail contacts, up-to-
date across all your devices (including a MacBook or other laptop,
iMac or PC or iPad) with the iCloud storage facility. Contacts are
stored in your iCloud account and pushed wirelessly to your other
iOS devices and computers that are set up with the same iCloud
account. To make sure that the iCloud and Contacts are working
together, go to Settings app on your iPhone and tap the iCloud
section on the left-hand side of the screen. On the right-hand side
of the screen, swipe the button next to the Contacts header to On.

If your iCloud storage is
insufficient to store your
Contact information, you
can purchase more

Assign a photo to a particular contact

1 Edit mode
Enter the Contacts app and tap
on a new or current contact.

2 Add a photo
If it is not visible, scroll to the Add
Photo box and tap on it.

3 Take or choose
Via the menu, choose to either
Take Photo or Choose Photo.

4 Insert photo
Use the iPhone to take a photo or
import from your photo archive.

Contacts

Fig 4 Tapping on a contact's address will open the Maps app and take you to that particular location

Integrate with other apps

It is possible to integrate the Contacts apps with other apps to form a seamless connection and also to allow you to perform tasks without having to pause to copy and paste from one app to another, or pause while one program is stopped and another opened. A good example is the Maps app.

If you open a current contact which features a full address, just tap on the address and this action will automatically open the Maps app (Fig 4). The Maps screen will then be displayed and that app will attempt to provide a visual indication of the address itself, giving you information on the location but also providing you with the opportunity to set up directions from your current location to that address. Similarly, if you list a website within the Contacts app,

Finished
When you're done, tap here and your contact will be stored on your phone with all the info you added

Extra fields
This field enables you to type whatever extra information you need, like Twitter names and job titles

Template
Type new information or edit the current information within the boxes. Scroll down to see more options

Delete info
When editing a contact, press on a red circle to reveal the Delete button, then tap it to clear the field

Before you share your contact, make sure all of the info is correct and edit it if you need to

tapping on it will open the Safari browser and the contents of that website will be displayed. You can also tap on an email address within your contact list to open the Mail app and create a new email to send to that person.

Share a contact

Within each completed Contact page, you have the ability to share the contact. This provides a quick and simple way of sharing details, which is ideal if a contact is packed with information that would take too long to copy or rewrite.

To share your contact, open your desired Contact page and look to the base of the profile. At the centre of three icons, is the Share Contact button. Two options then appear denoting how you can share that contact information. In this case, Email and Message. Tap on the Email option, for example, and a new email page will appear. Notice that a file icon also exists. This .vcf file contains all of the required information. When you email this file, your recipient can then load it into their Contacts app. All of the information will then be made available to the recipient too, so your Contacts app is a great way of networking.

Share via Message

1 Open Contact
Open a contact and scroll to the bottom until you see 'Share Contact'.

2 Share contact
Tap on Share Contact, select Message, enter the text and then send.

Email a contact card

1 Open Contacts
Open the Contacts app and select the contact of choice.

2 Scroll to Contacts
Look down to see the Share Contact option. Tap on it.

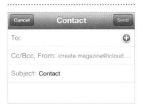

3 New email page
Tap on the Email option and a new email page will appear.

4 Complete email
Complete the email and send to pass on the .vcf file.

Phone

The Phone app does more than just make and receive calls

You'll use it to…

Make phone calls
Use the keypad to dial numbers

Check for missed calls
Use the Recents list to find out who's been calling you

Add contacts
Add new numbers to Contacts

Edit contacts
Make changes to existing contacts

Retrieve voicemails
Tap on Voicemail to check for spoken messages

Add favourites
Your Favourites get through right away when your iPhone is in Do Not Disturb mode

Fig 1 (above) The Phone app will probably be the most immediately familiar item on your new iPhone

Fig 2 (right) Phone provides you with a wealth of options while you are making a phone call

Make and receive calls

Just like an old-style mobile phone with a push-button keypad, the Phone app allows you to dial numbers from its software keypad (Fig 1), as well as use the # (hash) and * (star) keys in tandem with automated switchboards.

In-call options

If you make or receive a call, the Phone software presents you with a number of useful options (Fig 2). First off there's Mute. This lets you turn off the iPhone's microphone so the caller at the other end can't hear what you're saying, effectively putting the other caller on hold (works with iPhone 4 or later).

The Keypad option brings up a traditional-looking numeric keypad for those all-too-frequent occasions when you need to choose the options offered by an automated switchboard.

Speaker routes the incoming audio through the iPhone's speaker -- or, if you have one, a Bluetooth speaker or headset.

Contacts brings up the Contacts app, so you can refer to it quickly, which is handy when you need to pull up someone's number

quickly. To return to the call, simply tap the narrow green bar you'll see across the top of the iPhone's screen.

If the person you're calling has an iPhone 4 or later, tap the FaceTime button during a voice call, and you can make it into a FaceTime call. Finally, Add Call will allow you to connect another person to your current call.

View recent calls

Tap the Recents icon at the bottom of the screen and you'll see a list of your most recent calls: incoming, outgoing and missed. Missed calls are listed in red (the number of missed calls appears as a red 'badge' on the Recents icon). Outgoing calls have a 'handset' icon (with a diagonal arrow pointing away from it) under the contact's name, next to information about the phone number (mobile, home, work, and so on), while incoming calls you've answered have basic information about the caller's name and number. From this screen you can get more information by tapping the arrow button and call people back without having to leave the screen.

Use voicemail

If you have received a voicemail, you'll see an on-screen notification, with options either to close it or listen to the voicemail. If you closed the notification and now want to listen to the voicemail, tap the Phone app's icon, then the Voicemail icon in the bottom-right corner of the screen. With standard voicemail services, your iPhone will automatically dial your network's voicemail number, and you'll follow the spoken instructions from that point.

Tap on the arrow icon on a Recents listing to view more information, add or amend a contact

Set a reply message

1 Launch Settings To set a custom reply message, first tap Settings, then Phone.

2 Phone settings Tap Reply with Message, then on one of the default messages.

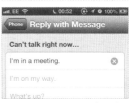

3 Set your message Replace the selected message with your own, and exit Phone then Settings.

4 Respond to incoming call with message Swipe the phone icon and tap Reply with Message.

Phone

Fig 3 The Phone app works together with Reminders so you remember to call people back

Set a reminder to call back

People don't always phone at convenient times. In fact, there are times when the only option – for the present – is to dismiss a call and phone them back later. However, how many times have you forgotten to make that important call because you've had so many other things happening around you? Well, fortunately for us, the Phone app works together with Reminders to make up for our shortcomings by reminding us to make that call. So when your iPhone starts to ring and you really can't take that call, just flick upwards on the small 'receiver' icon to the right of the Decline and Answer buttons and tap Remind Me Later. (Fig 3) You'll then be presented with four callback options: In 1 hour, When I leave, When I get home and Cancel. The first three options add an event to the

Do Not Disturb
The 'moon' icon in the upper part of the display indicates that Do Not Disturb is active

Voicemail
When you're waiting to receive a voicemail, you'll see a red 'badge' like this

* and # keys
Use these with the number keys to choose options interacting with an automated switchboard

Add contact
Tap this button to create a contact from a dialled number or add the number to an existing contact

Go to Reminders and tap on a call back reminder to call a contact directly from the reminder

Reminders app, and you'll be prompted to call back whenever you choose. If you've never set a location-based reminder before, you'll be asked for permission to use your current location.

Using Do Not Disturb

Ever forgotten to put your mobile on silent during the night, or forgotten to turn the sound back on in the morning and missed an important call? That's why Apple introduced a feature called Do Not Disturb into iOS 6.

Almost buried in Settings>Notifications, Do Not Disturb lets you silence calls, alerts and notifications (though not any alarms you've set in the Clock app) while your iPhone is locked. Better than that, you can schedule Do Not Disturb to operate only between certain times – during the night, for instance. That's all very well, but what if there are some people whose calls you always want to take? In that case you have a number of choices: you can allow calls through from contacts you've designated Favorites (see 'Contacts in Favorites' boxout), from everyone, no one, your stored contacts or from a pre-defined group of contacts (you'll need to log in to **www. icloud.com** to create a contacts group).

Allow Do Not Disturb to let repeated calls through

1 Settings Go to the Settings app, followed by Notifications and then Do Not Disturb.

2 Enable With Repeated Calls on, if the same number calls back within three minutes they'll get through.

Contacts in Favorites

1 Contacts First, go to the Phone app and tap on the Favorites option.

2 Addition Tap the + icon, and you will be taken to your list of contacts.

3 Choosing Search for the contact you want to add, and tap on 'Add to Favorites'.

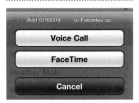

4 Done! Choose to add them as a Voice Call or FaceTime favourite, and you're finished.

Messages

Send messages and much more using this essential communication app

You'll use it to...

Send texts
Exchange text messages with other users over the mobile network

Share picture
Exchange pictures and videos from your iPhone and other sources over the mobile network

Use iMessages
Exchange unlimited messages with iOS and OS X Mountain Lion users

Share voice memos
Send memos from the Voice Memos app

Location information
Send details of a location from the iOS Maps or Google Maps apps

Fig 1 (above) The iPhone's beautiful screen lets you view your messages as a conversation

Fig 2 (right) Sending a message couldn't be easier. Simply tap the pencil and pad icon, enter a recipient and type in the text

View messages

Messages lets you send and receive text (sometimes called SMS) messages, as well as picture and video (MMS) messages over the mobile network (Fig 1). It also enables you to exchange unlimited messages with iOS and OS X Mountain Lion users over both Wi-Fi and mobile networks.

Send a text message

Tap the Messages icon. If there are no messages already in your inbox, a blank message will appear with 'New Message' displayed across the top of the screen with the on-screen QWERTY keyboard ready for action (Fig 2). Otherwise, tap the compose icon located in the top-right corner and a new message, plus the keyboard, will pop up.

The cursor will already be in the recipient field, so start typing the name of someone in your contacts list, and you'll see a list of suggestions that match what you've typed: choose one by tapping it. To add another recipient, tap the + to the right of the first recipient and Contacts will open: choose a contact as before by starting to type

their name. Alternatively, use the numbers on the keyboard to type in the recipient's phone number.

Tap in the text field, and use the keyboard to type your message. To add photos or video, tap the camera icon to the left of the text field and choose whether to use existing files or take new ones. When you've finished your message, tap Send.

Using iMessages

iMessages is a service from Apple that lets you send free, unlimited messages to devices that also happen to be running iOS (iPhone, iPad or iPod Touch) or OS X Mountain Lion (desktop or laptop Macs), over a mobile or Wi-Fi network. As with standard messaging, you can attach photos or videos. To set up iMessages, go to Settings>Messages, tap Use your Apple ID for iMessage, and sign in with your Apple ID. Tap Send & Receive>Add Another Email… to add an email address at which people can iMessage you.

Attach photos and files to a message

Your smartphone gives you a number of options for attaching files to messages. If you're in the Messages app, you can tap the small 'camera' icon located next to the text field. You'll then be presented with two options: either take a new photo or video, or use one of your existing files by selecting it from the Photos app. It's also possible to attach files to messages from within most of the other apps in which you've created or stored them, for example files in Photos or Voice Memos or links in Safari, for instance. To do this, select the file you want, tap the Share icon, and choose the way you want to share the file (in this case, as a message).

If a message fails you'll see the alert badge. Tap the badge to try and send the message again

Forward a message

1 Choose a conversation Open Messages and tap a conversation to open it.

2 Selecting a message Tap Edit, then select the message(s) you want to forward.

3 Edit your text Tap Forward, then add or amend your message as necessary.

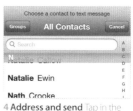

4 Address and send Tap in the To: field, add your recipient(s), and tap Send.

Fig 3 Messages lets you delete individual messages or entire threads

Delete messages

Though individual messages take up very little of your iPhone's internal memory, it's a good idea to prune the contents of your inboxes from time to time to keep them manageable and delete anything you no longer need stored on your device. Fortunately, the Messages app lets you delete either individual messages (Fig 3) or entire conversations, so you can keep only what you want to keep.

To delete individual messages within a thread, tap Messages, look through the list of conversations until you find the one you want, and tap it to show the individual messages within the conversation. Tap Edit and you'll notice a circle appear to the left of each individual message. Tap the circle next to each message you

Recipients field
Tap on the + to add more recipients from Contacts, or simply start typing their names

Message field
Compose your message in here – any attached files will also appear

Attach media button
Tap this button to add images – moving or still – to your message

Keyboard
Use the mini QWERTY keyboard to compose your message. To give your thumbs more room, rotate your iPhone 90 degrees

If you have problems with MMS, call your network and get them to refresh your settings

wish to delete, and tap Delete. If you change your mind, tap again to deselect a message.

To delete an entire thread, tap on Messages, but this time stay in Messages view. Tap Edit, then tap the icon to the left of the conversation you wish to delete (the one that looks like a no-entry sign). Tap Delete.

Send group messages

Sending messages to one recipient is all very well, but there are times when you may need to send out a group message to family, friends, colleagues and so on. Fortunately, Messages can handle messages with multiple recipients, too. Simply tap the New Message icon, start typing the names of any recipients you have stored in your contacts, and tap on their name once Messages brings up a list of names that match what you've typed. In some versions of iOS you might need to go into Settings>Messages and enable group messaging before sending a group MMS. It's also worth noting that if anyone replies to a group MMS from you, the reply will be sent only to you unless they add other recipients from their end.

Send a message to multiple recipients

1 Create a message Tap the New Message icon and enter your first recipient in the 'To' field.

2 Add more You can then tap the '+' icon to select another contact from the list that appears.

Search messages

1 Launch Messages To start your search, first launch the Messages app.

2 Start searching Swipe down until you see the search field at the top of the screen.

3 Enter text Tap your search term into the search field to find the message you're looking for.

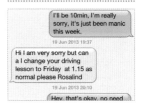

4 Open the message Tap the message in order to open and read it.

App Store

Your gateway to a rich source of apps is via the intuitive App Store – a bustling marketplace that is always open for business

You'll use it to…

Discover apps
Clearly defined sections help you find and discover exciting new apps

Search for apps
If you know the name of an app, enter it in the search field and you'll find it in seconds

Purchase apps
Buy and download apps to your iPhone

Gift apps
Send an app to someone special

Review apps
Give a little customer feedback

Get recommendations
Use the Genius feature to see what apps best suit you

Shop for apps

The App Store (Fig 1) will be your most-used iPhone app because it is here that you purchase and download content for your device. Thankfully, it is a very user-friendly environment where you can discover what's hot and make informed purchases in seconds.

Search the App Store

Considering that the shelves of the App Store have swelled to over 650,000 products, being able to find what you need quickly is of the ultimate importance – so it's just as well that there is an intuitive search engine on hand to help.

If you know the name of the app you're looking for then enter it into the Search field (Fig 2). As you type the letters, matches will instantly start being made with what you're typing. If you see what you want in the list of suggestions, then just tap on it to instantly go to that page. If you're not sure of what you're looking for, then there are plenty of handy pointers to steer you in the right direction. The 'Featured' section is a good starting point as it showcases all of the latest

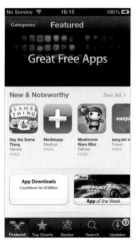

Fig 1 (above) The storefront is brimming with attractive offers and sections

Fig 2 (right) Start typing keywords into the search engine to find what you want

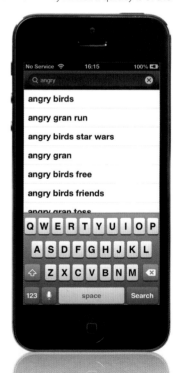

52

eye-catching apps of significance. From there you can use the Top Charts and Categories tabs at the bottom of the screen to see what's currently popular or begin searching in an area of interest.

Browse the Top Charts

If you start browsing the App Store without a clue of what to look for or where to go to look for it, then help is at hand. Using the touch icons at the bottom of the screen, tap on the Top Charts section and you will be presented with a rundown of the most popular apps available on the store – both full price and free. You can use this as a barometer to see what's hot in the world of apps and see if any popular apps jump out at you. Use swipe gestures to move through the different lists, which also includes a Top Grossing countdown, which is the apps that have earned the most through in-app purchases. Tap on any of the icons you see to get additional information about the app.

Genius

Like with iTunes, in which the Genius feature can be utilised to get song recommendations based on the music in your library, the App Store boasts a similar feature. While in the App Store, tap the Genius button at the bottom of the window and you'll be taken to a screen full of Genius recommendations based on the apps that are currently installed on your iPhone. The lay-out of this page is simple to digest as you can clearly see the app that inspired the recommendation, purchase the recommended app straight from the Genius page, or register that you are not interested by tapping the button underneath. Tap on the Categories icon to see your Genius results broken down into App Store sections.

You can browse all of the apps you have ever downloaded in the Purchased section

Redeem a gift card

1 Tap on Featured
Make sure that you're in the Featured section of the store.

2 Tap Redeem
Tap on the Redeem button at the bottom of the page.

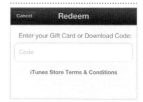

3 Tap on Code
Tap on the Code field and then enter your code.

4 Redeem your app
Tap Redeem and your gifted app will subsequently download.

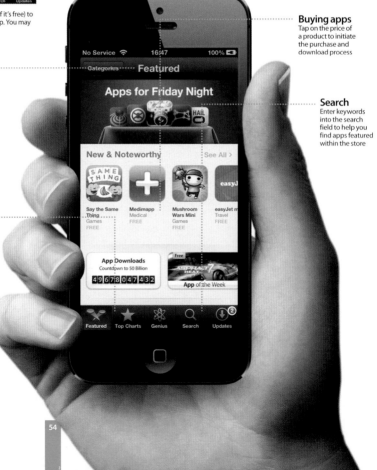

Fig 3 Tap on the price (or 'Free' if it's free) to purchase and download the app. You may have to enter your Apple ID

Purchase an app

Being the only source of gaining apps for your iPhone, the App Store is, as you would expect, a quick and easy way to shop for new apps, and purchasing them really couldn't be simpler. You will already be logged into the App Store with your registered Apple ID, which should have your billing details attached.

   If you haven't already added the details of a valid credit or debit card for your app funding then tap on the Featured page at the App Store, scroll down to the bottom and then tap on your Apple ID. Select 'View Apple ID' from the menu and then tap on the Payment Information option. You can now select a card type and enter all of the required information so that all app purchases will

Buying apps
Tap on the price of a product to initiate the purchase and download process

Search
Enter keywords into the search field to help you find apps featured within the store

Featured apps
All the latest significant new additions to the App Store will be showcased in the main shop window under Featured

Store sections
You will be able to access specific stores for Top Charts, Featured, Genius recommendations and more by tapping these buttons

No reviews for the current version? Then look further back by tapping on the 'All Versions' button

be made using that card. Now you can tap on the price of an app (Fig 3) and then complete the purchase by inputting your Apple ID password. You will still need to enter your Apple ID password when downloading free apps, but you don't have to assign a credit or debit card to do so.

Review and rate apps

App feedback is good, not only because feedback – good or bad – gets back to the developer and lets them know how the public is receiving their apps and how they can make them better. It also provides information for your fellow iPhone users to help them make informed decisions on whether to buy a particular app or not, so if you have the time and the inclination, then why not leave your own mini app review?

To do this, tap on an app (it has to be an app you own for you to be able to review it) to access its info page and then select the Reviews tab to see the current ratings, complete with star ratings and a chart showing other customers ratings of the app. You can write your own review for the product by tapping on the Write a Review link that is situated under the Customer Reviews chart. A

Submit a review of an app

1 Write a Review
Tap on the row of stars to rate an app that you own out of five.

2 Get critical
Tap on the Write a Review link and then submit your thoughts.

Recommend an app

1 Tap on The Share button
Go to an app's info page and tap the Share button (a box and arrow).

2 Email
If you tap Mail, then you can send an email with the app's info.

3 Message
Tapping Message enables you to send an iMessage.

4 Tweet
If you have a Twitter account set up, you can also tweet about it.

Delete an app

1 Press and hold
Press down on an app icon until they start jiggling.

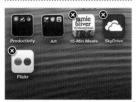

2 Tap the 'X'
Tap on the 'X' that appears next to the icon.

3 Deleting apps
A dialogue box will then appear, so tap on Delete.

4 Tap Home
When the app has gone, tap the Home button to return to normal.

To rename a folder, tap the 'X' at the end of the title bar and then rename it whatever you want

box will then appear with spaces for a review title and your text. Once done, hit Submit to get your review published on the page.

Update your apps

Apps are constantly evolving, improving and updating, but rather than charge you for an app, get customer feedback and then charge you again when an update comes out, the updates are always completely free once you have bought the product. What's more, you don't have to trawl the App Store to see if your favourite apps have updates because there's a section dedicated to them, which is accessible through the aptly named Updates tab at the bottom of the interface. If you have any updates ready, you'll see a red bubble with the number of apps that need updating inside it.

Tap on this and all of the apps that you have installed on your device that have been updated will be listed. You can then scroll down the list and tap the Update button next to a particular app to update it. Alternatively, you can tap on the Update All button in the top-right corner of the screen to automatically download all applicable updates in one fell swoop.

Create a folder of apps

1 Press and hold
Press down on an app icon until they all start jiggling.

2 Stack them
Drag the icon on top of another icon and then release.

Manage your apps

Whenever you purchase an app it will be downloaded to your device and appear in an available slot on one of your Home screens. However, the position it takes up upon download isn't set in stone and you can move your apps around freely and place them wherever you want – even creating new folders to store them all in.

To move apps around, press and hold on an app icon until they all start to shake (and an 'X' appears next to each icon that you can press to delete the app) then press and hold on the icon and move it to a new position. If you want to move the app to a different Home Screen, drag it to the side of the screen (Fig 4) and within a second, the next or previous Home Screen will appear (depending on the side of the screen you move the app to). Place the app where you want it to sit and then release. To create folders for apps, simply drag one app icon onto another and a folder will form.

Fig 4 Drag an app icon to the sides to move it to a different screen

Update All
To get all available updates, tap on the Update All button in the top-left corner

Manual update
Tap on the Update button next to a listed app in order to manually update it

Update info
The details of what each update contains will appear alongside the name of the app

Updates tab
A red bubble on the Updates tab tells you that you have apps that need updating

iTunes

Let your iPhone entertain you with music, movies and TV shows – all of which can be bought right here

You'll use it to…

Browse for items
Sections make it easy to find new content and great deals

Purchase media
Buying new music and movies is easy

Discover new media
Search and roam for interesting items

Gift items
Buy and send a gift to a loved one

Make use of Genius
Get artist recommendations and create smart playlists

Get educated
Get access to a wealth of study materials with the iTunes U app

Buy music & movies

Although there are links to the respective sections of the iTunes Store within the Music and Videos apps, you can access the store direct from its own app on the Home screen and browse for content at your leisure. And there is plenty to explore (Fig 1)…

The Categories in iTunes

Navigating your way around the iTunes Store is made easy by a series of tabs at the bottom of the screen that allow you to breeze freely to the various store categories that include Music, Films, TV Programmes, Audiobooks and more (Fig 2). Tap on a category to access a front-page relating to that particular category that is packed full of featured offers and attractions.

If you have bought things previously from the iTunes Store on other iOS devices (like iPhone or iPod touch) then, thanks to Apple's iCloud service, you will be able to re-download them again onto your iPhone – just tap on the Purchased category (found under 'More') then on the 'Not on this iPhone' tab at the top of

Fig 1 (above) The iTunes Store is a thriving hive of digital entertainment

Fig 2 (right) Use the tabs at the bottom of the interface to jump straight to the various store categories

the page and then choose a song and tap on the cloud icon. If you are currently downloading content from the iTunes Store then you will be able to track the progress of your purchases by tapping on the Downloads category. This is also found under the More section where you can also see Audiobooks and even Ringtones that you have download. Note that this is also the location of the Genius icon.

Rent & buy a movie

Search for & sample a song

One of the good things about the iTunes Store is that it allows you to try before you buy. First of all, search for an album or artist you may be interested in by tapping the search field in the top corner of the screen. Now tap on an album and then tap on a track name to listen to a sizeable chunk to determine if it is what you're looking for. You can end the preview at any time by either tapping on another song or tapping the Stop button in the middle of the playback wheel. You'll also notice the three-lined icon in the top right corner, this is the History icon and allows users to look back at their preview listening past.

Download songs

Purchasing and downloading songs from the iTunes Store is a quick and easy process that can be done in seconds. We have already explored how you can search for songs and preview tracks, and if you decide that you would like to go ahead with the purchase then tap on the price and it will turn into a green 'Buy Song' button.

If you then wish to go ahead with the purchase, you will be prompted to enter your Apple ID password before the track will start downloading – this is a security measure to ensure that you don't buy items by tapping on them accidentally. You can track

1 Find a film
Search the Films section until something takes your fancy.

2 Get info
Tap on the name of the film to open up its info box.

3 Watch a preview
Tap on the Trailer movie to get a sneak peek at the film.

4 Buy or rent?
Tap on the Buy or Rent buttons, sign in and download your movie.

If you are lucky enough to be gifted a redeem code, scroll down the Music page and tap Redeem

Fig 3 The iTunes U app is downloadable from the App Store

the progress of this by tapping on the Downloads category at the bottom of the screen.

Introducing iTunes U

If you are currently studying at school or higher education then the iTunes Store also provides a wealth of materials to help make learning easier. This service, called iTunes U, was available as a store category, accessible via one of the tabs at the bottom of the screen in iOS 5. But since the release of iOS 6, it has migrated out of the iTunes app into its own standalone app that operates exactly like Music, Videos, iBooks and Newsstand in allowing you to jump straight to the applicable section of the iTunes Store from within.

Buying
Tap on the price of a product to start the purchase and download process. Ensure you are logged in and have funding set up

Featured sections
All of the latest significant new additions to the iTunes Store will be showcased in the main shop window and heavily flagged

Search the store
Enter keywords into the search field to find specific artists, songs, movies or programmes featured within the store

Store sections
You will be able to access specific stores for Music, Films, TV Programmes, Audiobooks and more at the bottom of the screen

It will cost £21.99 a year to use iTunes Match, so consider how much use you will get out of it

The iTunes U part of the store is laid out like the other sections, with its own Featured, Top Charts and Categories sections (Fig 3), and you can also use the search bar to find what you want. Once you have found a set of study materials that you are interested in, tap on the title to open the info page and then hit the Subscribe button. The materials will then be downloaded and populate the shelves of your iTunes U app, where you can access and browse them at your leisure whenever you are ready to start studying.

iTunes Match

As iTunes now works in perfect harmony with Apple's iCloud service, any music that you purchase, regardless of which device you're using to make the purchase, will be automatically pushed to your other iOS 6 devices.

iTunes Match (which requires an annual subscription) is an extension of this service which matches the music on your computer, that has been imported from CDs, to its digital iTunes Store counterpart, and stores it all in your iCloud ready for use. iTunes determines which songs in your collection are available in

Enabling iTunes Match

1 Subscribe
On your computer, launch iTunes, click iTunes Match and subscribe.

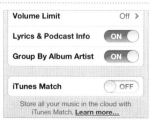

2 Go to Settings
On your iPhone, go to the Music Settings and enable iTunes Match.

Pause a download

1 Download content
Start downloading content, such as a song or audiobook.

2 Go to Downloads
A number appears next to the Downloads tab. Tap on it.

3 Tap to pause
Tap on the pause button to halt the download process.

4 Resume download
When you are ready to resume downloading, tap the arrow.

Pre-order an album

1 Go to Music section
Navigate to the Music section of iTunes by tapping the Music tab.

2 Pre-Orders
Look out for pre-orders advertised on the iTunes Store.

3 Access info
Open an item's info page and you will see a pre-order button.

4 Tap to pre-order
Tap it, enter your ID and the album will download when it's out.

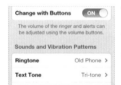

When you buy alert tones they will be added to the Sounds section in General Settings

the iTunes Store and any music with a match is automatically added to iCloud for you to listen to at any time, on any device. Since there are more than 20 million songs in the iTunes Store, chances are your music is already in iCloud.

iTunes in the Cloud

With iCloud, the music that you purchase in iTunes appears automatically on all of your mobile iOS devices and Macs running OS X Mountain Lion. You can also download your past iTunes purchases where you want, when you want. iCloud can automatically download new music purchases to all your devices over Wi-Fi – or over a cellular network if your iPhone has that capability. Which means you can buy a song from iTunes on your iPhone at home, and find it waiting for you on your iPhone during your morning commute, all without even having to sync.

Any music you have purchased in the past will also be easily accessible. Simply tap on the 'Purchased' tab and you will be able to view an alphabetical list of all of your past purchases. If one of the items isn't currently on your iPhone then highlight it and then tap on the cloud icon that is next to the song name. The song will

Finding tones

1 The More menu
Tap the 'More' menu in the top bar, then select 'Tones'.

2 Purchase tones
Browse products and then purchase tones as you would other media.

instantly start downloading to your device and will then be playable through the Music app (Fig 4).

You can also subscribe to iTunes Match, which will match songs in the iTunes catalogue with those ripped from CDs on your computer and allow you to access them any time you want.

The Tones Store

iTunes includes the Tones Store, which provides access to a variety of different ringtones and sound effects (Fig 5). You will find this section of the Store under the More icon. When searching for specific items using the smart search engine, the chances are that the app will throw up ringtones as suggestions so you can jump straight to that product. Purchasing tones is easy and uses the same process as if you were buying music or film. Simply tap on a price next to a product to make the purchase and download the product.

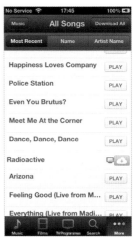

Fig 4 Re-download past iTunes purchases on your current device for free

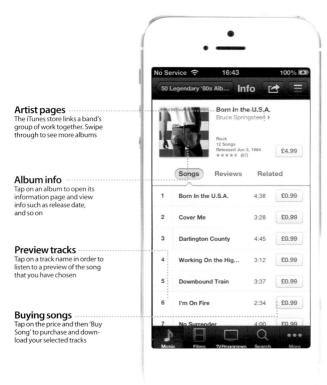

Artist pages
The iTunes store links a band's group of work together. Swipe through to see more albums

Album info
Tap on an album to open its information page and view info such as release date, and so on

Preview tracks
Tap on a track name in order to listen to a preview of the song that you have chosen

Buying songs
Tap on the price and then 'Buy Song' to purchase and download your selected tracks

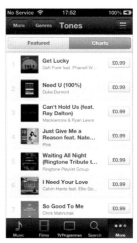

Fig 5, The Tones Store contains ringtone versions of the iTunes Chart, so you can get all the latest tracks

Music

The Music app enables you to belt out the hits in style on your iPhone

You'll use it to…

Play music
A simple set of controls let you belt out your tunes

Make playlists
Create new playlists on the fly quickly and easily

Go shopping
Access the iTunes Store to grab new songs

Use Genius
Allow the app to create playlists for you

Access podcasts
Play all of your downloaded podcasts

Searching content
Find what you want, when you want to listen to it

Fig 1 (above) You can view your music by Songs, Artist or Album in the Music interface and even visit the iTunes store

Fig 2 (right) You can re-download past purchases that aren't on your iPhone as everything is tracked by iCloud

Listen to music on the go

Replacing what was the iPod app, Music is where you can listen to all of the top tunes that you have synced or purchased on your iPhone. Through this app you can listen to tracks, create playlists and shop for new music through the iTunes store (Fig 1).

Import songs

There are numerous ways to import music to play on your iPhone. The most direct route is by purchasing it straight from the iTunes store on your device, and you can do this by tapping on the Store button in the top left corner of the Music interface and then browsing the store. While in the iTunes store, you can also tap on the Purchased tab at the bottom of the interface and this will list all of the music that you have bought previously on other devices.

Thanks to the power of iCloud, all of your previous purchases are tracked (Fig 2), so select a track and then tap the cloud icon to re-download it on your current device. Of course, you can also import songs by connecting your device to your computer and syncing through iTunes or, alternatively, opening iTunes on your computer, highlighting songs in your music library and then manually dragging them to your iPhone in the left-hand column. The bottom line is you and your music need be apart no longer, no matter which device you download it on.

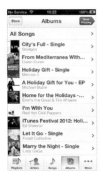

Playing your music

First and foremost, the Music app is there to enable you to play and listen to music on your iPhone, and the controls for doing this are simple to get to grips with. Start off by choosing music to listen to, whether it be searching by artist, album or even your own custom playlists, selecting a tab at the bottom of the screen and navigating to a song, then tap on it to start playing it. The controls at the top of the interface allow you to play/pause the current song and skip to the next or previous songs.

Add lyrics from iTunes

If you want to sing along to your favourite songs through the Music app then there is a way to get lyrics displayed on screen while the song is playing, but this involves using iTunes on your computer.

Start off by searching online for the song lyrics and then copy them by highlighting them and pressing Cmd (Mac) or Ctrl (Windows)+C. Now open iTunes, right-click on the corresponding song and choose the 'Get Info' option from the menu. In the window that appears, click on the Lyrics tab and then paste the copied lyrics into the window (Cmd/Ctrl+V) and tap OK. You will now need to delete the original song off of your iPhone and then re-sync it with iTunes to get the lyrics onto your iPhone.

If viewing album art when playing songs, skip tracks by swiping left or right across the screen

Rate your albums

1 Start playing
Select an album from your library and then start playing it.

2 Tap Icon
Tap on the icon in the top right corner of the Now Playing screen.

3 Track List
A full album track list appear complete with a row of dots.

4 Tap the dots
Tap the row of dots above the track listing to rate out of five.

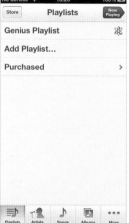

Genius playlists

A Genius playlist is a collection of songs from your library that work well together and you can create Genius playlists in iTunes on your computer and sync them to your iPhone or directly on the device itself. Genius has a knack of stringing similar songs together, creating smooth playlists by compiling tracks you perhaps never thought to place side by side in a running order – perfect for a party.

To use Genius on iPhone, first turn on Genius in iTunes on your computer and then sync the iPhone with iTunes. Genius mixes are synced automatically (unless you manually manage your music and decide which mixes you want to sync in iTunes). Back on the iPhone, you can play the mixes by tapping on the Playlists tab at the

Fig 3 Access your Genius playlists by tapping on the Playlists tab at the bottom of the screen

Song info
At the top of the screen you'll be able to see the artist, song title and the album it's from

Advanced controls
The top bar also features controls to repeat songs, shuffle songs, scrub through songs, use Ping and add the song to a Genius playlist

Playback controls
You can play/pause and skip songs using the simple set of controls in the top-left corner of the screen

Volume control
You can pump up the volume by dragging this slider to the right position. Press and hold and move the slider

You can scrub through songs by pressing on the line on the top bar and then dragging it

bottom of the Music app interface and selecting the Genius playlist (Fig 3). If you wish to refresh a Genius Playlist, open the playlist on your iPad and tap Refresh. If you want to make a new Genius playlist using a different song, simply tap the Genius atom icon on the top bar when the song is playing and a new playlist will be created.

Manage your playlists

Creating and managing playlists on your iPhone is easy through the Music app. As well as creating new playlists from scratch, you can also edit playlists that have been synced across from iTunes in order to update them or make subtle tweaks here and there.

To create a new playlist, simply tap on the Playlists tab and then tap the Add Playlist option in the list. Give your new playlist a name, tap Save and then start adding songs from your library by either tapping on the song itself or the '+' icon next to it. When you have finished adding, tap Done and your playlist will be complete. If you wish to edit an existing playlist, select it from the Playlists page and then tap the Edit button. You can now delete songs by tapping the '-' icon next to each song or change the order by holding on the list icon next to each song and dragging it up or down.

Create a playlist

1 Tap on New
On the Playlists screen, tap New, name your playlist and then tap Save.

2 Add songs
Add songs by tapping on a song name or the '+' icon.

Delete songs

1 Locate the song
Use the tabs at the bottom of the screen to locate the song.

2 Swipe left
Swipe left on a song and a Delete option will appear. Tap it.

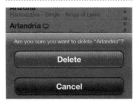

3 Instant erase
Confirm your choice and the song will disappear.

4 Delete entire albums
Swipe on albums in your list and delete them like songs.

Videos

The Videos app lets you watch movies and TV shows anywhere on your iPhone

You'll use it to…

Watch videos
Watch films, music videos and TV shows on your iPhone

Shop for content
Access the iTunes Store in-app to shop for videos

Stream to Apple TV
Beam your videos straight to the big screen

Stream video from your computer
Watch your computer video library remotely on your iPhone

Watch anywhere
Take your device with you watch videos anywhere

Manage your movies
Sync from you computer and delete when watched

Watch TV shows and movies on iPhone
You can use your iPhone to watch movies, music videos and TV shows, transforming it into a mobile multiplex to view what you want, on demand. Using the Videos app is easy, so sit back, relax and enjoy the show.

Rent & buy from iTunes
Just like the Music app, Videos features a launch pad to the iTunes Store, in this case the visual entertainment section – where you can shop for films to rent or films to buy outright. Simply tap the Store button in the top-left corner of the main Videos interface to be warped to the iTunes Store and then use the search field to find what you want.

When you have found a film, tap on the poster next to the title and a new window will appear that provides a plot synopsis, credits, details and user reviews. More importantly it also features a button that allows you to preview the movie through your Videos app

Fig 1 If you're unsure about a film, you can watch a trailer to get a taste for the movie

(Fig 1) and options to buy or rent the movie. If you're buying then the system is the same as purchasing music or apps – just tap 'Buy' and the film will download to your device.

Renting is slightly different – you still download it, but it will expire after a certain number of days and, once you start a movie, you have a limited amount of time to finish watching it. It does mean you will never have to pay a late fee though!

Import videos from your computer

If you don't want to buy directly from the iTunes Store through the app then you can also import videos from your computer via iTunes. Simply connect your device and then click on the Movies section under your Library to view all of the movies on your machine. Now you can either drag the film to your iPhone in the sidebar or perform a sync to get your flicks onto your device.

Playing your videos

As with music, playing videos on your device is easy. From the main Videos app screen, with a list of all your video downloads filling the screen, broken down into sections depending on whether it's TV show, music video or, movie. Users can also use the Search bar at the top of the screen to quickly jump to specific titles that you're looking for within the app.

When the video is launched, a simple set of controls at the bottom of the screen allow you to play or pause the action, skip chapters and adjust the volume. You can also scrub through the action by swiping along the bar at the top of the screen, before leaving the video at any point by tapping the Done button in the top left hand corner of the screen.

Use the on-screen controls to tweak volume as well as scrub through your video as you wish

Change scrub speed

1 Tap scrub bar
Press your finger down on the dot situated on the scrub bar.

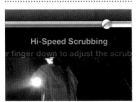

2 Scrub rate
The scrub rate will be displayed (either high or half-speed).

3 Swipe down
Slide your finger down to change to the alternate speed.

4 Start scrubbing
You can now slide your finger along the bar at the selected rate.

Videos

Fig 2 Viewing movies and TV shows through your device is simple through the Videos app

Fig 3 You can access your computer movie library to watch on your iPhone

Home Sharing

With Home Sharing, you can play movies and TV shows on your iPhone from the iTunes library on your Mac or PC. To use this feature, both your iPhone and your computer need to be on the same Wi-Fi network and, on your computer, you must have iTunes open and running. In iTunes, click on the Advanced menu and then turn on Home Sharing and ensure that both your computer and iPhone are logged in and using the same Apple ID.

To ensure that you are logged into the same Apple ID on your iPhone, go to Settings, tap on the Music or Videos sections and then log your details under the Home Sharing section. Once the system has been set up, a new tab will appear at the top of your Videos interface called Shared. Tap on this and then choose to access your

End viewing
If you wish to stop watching, tap the Done button and resume where you left off later

Rewind
Press and hold the dot on this bar, and by sliding it to the left you can rewind the action

Screen size
Tapping this button will make the video fill the screen. Tap it again to return to the original dimensions

Playback controls
Simple controls let you play and pause the action, skip backwards or forwards through chapters and adjust the volume

With your iPhone, you can mirror the screen on a TV wirelessly using AirPlay Mirroring and Apple TV

computer's library (Fig 3). Now simply select something to watch, sit back and enjoy. To deactivate this service, click on the Advanced menu on your computer again and then turn off Home Sharing to instantly sever the connection.

AirPlay

If you have an Apple TV system in your home then you can stream video content from your iPhone to your TV wirelessly using AirPlay. This is easy to set up and means that you can use your iPhone to shop for movies to buy or rent and then use your device as a remote control to play them on your big TV screen.

To start streaming video with AirPlay, start playing a video on your iPhone and then tap the AirPlay button. Next, choose your Apple TV from the list of AirPlay devices and then select it to start beaming the video across. If the AirPlay button doesn't appear or your Apple TV doesn't appear in the list, check to make sure that both devices are connected to the same wireless network. You can also stream videos using various cables, including AV cables and VGA Adapters. Being able to watch your videos on the big screen is a great advantage of having an iPhone, and being able to see all your videos, including home shot ones, is a nice option to have.

Streaming videos with AirPlay

1 Start playback
Start watching a video, tap on the AirPlay icon, then tap Apple TV.

2 Nothing on iPhone
While your video is playing on Apple TV, your iPhone will display this screen.

Delete videos

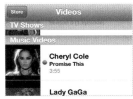

1 Locate video
Find a video that you no longer want on your device.

2 Press and hold
Press down on the video until an 'X' appears in the corner.

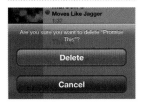

3 Tap to delete
Tap on the 'X' icon and a message will appear asking if you're sure.

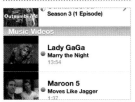

4 Instant removal
Tap Delete and then video will be deleted from your device.

Safari

Safari

The Safari app makes browsing the internet on your iPhone both quick and simple

You'll use it to…

Browse the web
Trawl your favourite sites on your iPhone

Keep tabs
Keep your favourite pages open

Read clearly
Read stories in a clean, uncluttered Safari Reader window

Keep a Reading List
Save your favourite stories to read whenever you want – even offline

Share webpages
Tweet or add pages to your Facebook status on the fly

Add links
Create handy Home screen shortcuts for your favourite webpages

Surf with ease

Browsing the internet on your iPhone is a simple and intuitive experience made easy by the touch-screen interface and simple gestures that mean you can tap on links to access them, pinch and expand your fingers to zoom and swipe your finger up or down to scroll the pages. The portability of the iPhone also means you can surf the net anywhere you have a Wi-Fi connection (Fig 1).

Browse the web

To start browsing the web on your iPhone, ensure that your device is connected to a Wi-Fi network (which you can do in your Settings app) and then launch Safari and tap on the address field or search window. Use the pop-up keyboard to enter a URL or a search keyword and then the page should load in the main window.

A simple interface makes it easy to bookmark your favourite pages. At the bottom of the screen is an share icon that you can touch to bring up a list of options (Fig 2). We'll come to some of these later but the 'Bookmark' option provides everything you need to store your favourite pages for easy access.

Fig 1 (above) Trawling the internet is second nature on an iPhone

Fig 2 (right) Tap the share button to access a wide range of options

Once you have added a bookmark, you can rename it whatever you want. So rather than store it as the long, often convoluted web address, you can shorten it to something snappier. Tap on the Bookmarks option and you'll be able to store it in the Bookmarks Menu – accessible from this list – or save in the Bookmarks Bar, which has it's own icon next to Share, from which you can look through the list of all your saved sites.

Browse with tabs

Tabbed web browsing allows users to keep up to nine webpages open simultaneously. These pages will be arranged as tabs in their own window, found in the bottom right corner of the screen. The number of tabs you currently have opened is included in the icon, and you can swipe between pages with a single gesture, seeing a full screen preview of the page in the process so you know exactly what's on the page. Adding new tabs is easy. While on the tabs screen, press the 'New Page' icon in the bottom left corner to open a new window and instantly store the page you were on as a tab.

iCloud tabs

With the introduction of iOS 6, browsing the internet on your iPhone just got much easier – now you can start browsing on one device and continue exactly where you left off on another.

With iCloud tabs, any tabs that you have open on your iPhone will be viewable on any other device that is running iOS 6, like an iPad or Mac (as long as it is running OS X Mountain Lion) and vice versa. All you have to do is tap the Bookmarks icon at the bottom of the screen, choose iCloud Tabs and any tabs that you have open

Choose 'Add to Home Screen' from the Share menu to turn a webpage into an app icon

Enable iCloud Tabs

1 Activate iCloud
Log into the same iCloud account on all of your devices.

2 Open Safari
Open up the Safari app and load a new tab.

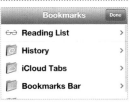

3 Choose iCloud tabs
Under the Bookmarks icon, tap the iCloud Tabs option.

4 Tap on link
These are the open tabs on your other devices. Tap to access.

Pakistan votes in landmark election

1 hour ago

Voting is under way across Pakistan in landmark national and provincial elections.

The vote marks Pakistan's first transition from one civilian government to another in its 66-year history.

However, the run-up to the election has been marred by violence in which more than 100 people have been killed.

A bomb blast in the port city of

Fig 3 The Reader option lets you view a cleaner version of certain webpages

on your other devices (which are connected to the same iCloud account) will be selectable.

Safari Reader

Safari Reader is a relatively new feature that enables web articles to be displayed without ads or clutter, so you can read away without distractions. Not all webpages support this feature, but those that do are instantly apparent because a small 'Reader' icon will be displayed in the address bar at the top of the window.

When you see the Reader icon, tap on it to activate the Safari Reader feature and a new window will be opened that strips away all of the ads, links and unnecessary clutter to leave pure, simple text that can be read and digested easily. You can also change the font

Search engine
By default, the Google search engine is built into Safari, but you can change this in Settings

Tabbed pages
Tap on the layered box icon to keep your current page as a tab and open a new tab. You can keep up to nine pages tabbed

Address bar
If you know a website address then type it directly in here. If the page is available for Safari Reader, then the Reader icon will appear in the bar

Sharing options
Tapping this icon will allow you to add bookmarks, add to Reading List, add to Home Screen, email links , Tweet and Print

To delete pages from your Reading List, swipe left on the list and tap on the Delete button

through Safari Reader to make it even bigger and easier to read. To do this, tap the font icon in the top-left corner of the Safari Reader page and choose between the default or enhanced font (Fig 3). When you have finished reading an article through Safari Reader, simply tap on the Done icon to return to the original page and continue your browsing as normal.

Offline Reading List

Reading List was first introduced with the release of iOS 5 and it allowed you to save links to webpages for you to read later. However, this was essentially just a glorified bookmark system and it was only with the release of iOS 6 that this feature became truly useful. When you add pages to your Reading List now, Safari will save the entire webpage, not just the link, so you can catch up on your reading even when you can't connect to the internet.

To save an article to your Reading List, tap the sharing icon at the bottom of the screen on the main Safari window while the page you wish to save is displayed in the main window and then select the Add to Reading List option. To then access the pages saved to your Reading List, tap the book icon at the bottom of the window,

Add a page to your Reading list

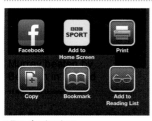

1 Tap sharing icon
While on a page, tap the sharing icon and choose 'Add to Reading List'.

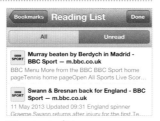

2 Access your list
Tap on the bookmarks icon and choose Reading List.

Clear your history

1 Go to Bookmarks
Tap the book icon and then go to the History section.

2 Clear History
Tap the Clear History button to erase all of your previous visits.

3 Go to Settings
Launch your Settings app and then tap on the Safari section.

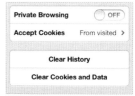

4 Clear out
Tap options to Clear History and Clear Cookies and Data.

Safari

Fig 4 You can trim the names of your bookmarks before adding them to your bar

tap Bookmarks and then you will see the Reading List section at the top of your bookmarks list.

Bookmarks bar

As we have explored, there are numerous ways to save and store your favourite webpages to keep them close at hand – and one of the best ways is to save them to your Bookmarks Bar. This is essentially a spread of bookmarked sites that run across the top of your Safari web browser on things like Mac or iPad, underneath the address bar, that you can access far quicker than scrolling through your Bookmarks Menu. On iPhone it appears under the Bookmark icon.

To add a new bookmark to your Bookmarks bar, tap the sharing icon at the bottom of the screen and then choose the Add

Social interaction
If you are logged into Twitter and Facebook accounts you can post links to pages in-app

Add to Home Screen
By selecting this option you can turn webpages into app icons on your Home screen for quick access

Add to Reading List
With iOS 6 you can now save entire webpages to read offline later when you don't have a connection

Sharing screen
You're presented with a number of other options from the ones mentioned above, including the ability to print and bookmark

Fig 5 Share anything interesting you find on the web nearly instantly thanks to Safari links to Facebook and Twitter

To share a page via Twitter or Facebook, sign into your account(s) in the Settings app

Bookmark option. You can then rename it and then choose a destination to save it to (Fig 4). Tap the Bookmarks section and then select Bookmarks Bar and when you are happy to add the site, tap Save and the name of the site will appear at the top of your Safari window for easy access when you pick up another of your devices.

Share a website

Sometimes you may see something on the web that amazes or outrages you to the extent that you simply have to share it with others. Thankfully, Safari provides a few options to quickly share your online discoveries with others. These options are all accessible through the sharing icon, situated at the bottom of the screen which, as we have already discovered, is your gateway to a host of Safari features. From this menu you can select the Mail Link to this Page option, Tweet or Print (Fig 5). The first option enables you to send an email of the page link directly out from Safari without having to copy and paste anything into the Mail app. The title of the link forms the subject of the email and you will be able to add your own message in the main email window, which also contains a link to the site that the recipients can click or tap on.

Sharing a webpage

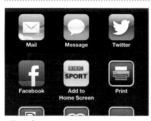

1 Tap share
Tap the sharing icon and then choose a method of sharing.

2 Pass it on
You will be able to share the page without leaving the Safari app.

Enable private browsing

1 Go to Settings
Quit Safari and, from your Home screen, launch your Settings app.

2 Tap Safari
To go the Safari section from the list on the screen.

3 Go private
Under Privacy, turn on the Private Browsing option.

4 Private browsing
In Private Browsing mode, the interface of Safari will be black.

Mail

Mail

With Apple's versatile Mail app you can send emails and receive every message from every account into one handy inbox

Link accounts
You can activate the Mail app with any valid email address and password

Send and receive
Keep up to date with email arrivals and quickly send out new messages

Manage accounts
Add as many accounts as you like

Organise your messages
Store and save messages safely away

Find emails easily
Mark certain people as VIPs to access their emails from a special mailbox

Get emails quick
No need to press anything, just get your emails downloaded automatically

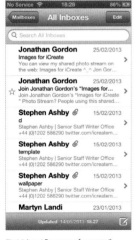

Fig 1 (above) Every one of your email accounts, together at last

Fig 2 (right) Once you have set up an account, go to the Settings app to link more accounts to your Mail app

Manage your email

Your iPhone's built-in Mail app is brilliant for sending and receiving emails, so you don't have to carry a laptop everywhere with you to keep in touch! You can also get all of your different email accounts linked to the app so every email from every account is streamed into one handy inbox (Fig 1), so you'll never have to worry about missing an important one again.

Link an account

If you are using the Mail app for the first time then you will need to set up and tether an account to the app. This is a quick and easy process that requires no more than a valid and active email address and an account password (Fig 2). Once set up, select your account in the 'Inboxes' section of the Mailboxes area and then all new messages will instantly be downloaded for that account. You can determine when all new emails are pushed from the servers to your mailbox by launching your Settings app, tapping on the Mail, Contacts, Calendars section and then selecting the Fetch

New Data option. Activate the Push function and then determine exactly when the messages will be received. To ensure that you get all new mail as soon as possible, tick the 'Manually' option to get all new mail pushed straight to your device as and when. Your device will also now automatically scan for new mail when you launch the app.

Mail and Notifications

One of the many good things about the Mail app is that you don't have to manually press a button to download new messages from the server, it just happens automatically whenever you open the app. What's more, if you have the Mail app listed in your Notification Center then you will get alerts on your screen whenever a new email is received. You should also ensure that Mail is activated in iCloud Settings so that all of your messages – received and read – are synced to all of your devices. This means that you will never be apart from all your email, across accounts, no matter which device you pick up. It's one of the best productivity and organisation tools around.

Write and send an email

Writing and sending emails is easy through the intuitive Mail app interface. To compose and send an email, simply tap on the pen and paper icon in the bottom-right corner of the Mail interface and a blank email will appear. Fill in the recipient's email address, enter a subject and some body text and then hit the 'Send' button. You can also mail out attachments, such as photos and documents from within the other respective apps by tapping on the sharing icon (which is represented by a small rectangle icon with an arrow in it).

You can move emails to different mailboxes by tapping Edit then marking emails to move

Use All Inboxes

1 Set up multiple accounts
Go to Mail, Contacts, Calendars in Settings and add accounts.

2 Add accounts
Select the account type and enter the email address and password.

3 Open Mail
Launch your Mail app and then tap on the 'All Inboxes' option.

4 Get all mail
All of your mail from all of your accounts will be redirected here.

Manage multiple accounts

It's very rare these days that folk just have one email address. At the very least most would have a work and a personal account. The Mail app is versatile enough to incorporate virtually any type of email account within a few easy steps and, handily, you can stream all of your mail from all of your accounts into onto main inbox, making it easy to track all aspects of your life simultaneously. To add a new account, launch your Settings app and then go to the Mail, Contacts, Calendars section.

Under the Accounts section at the top of the page you'll see the option to 'Add Account…' (Fig 3), tap this and then choose the type of account you will be adding. Once you have selected the account, enter a name, email address and password for that account and, after a few seconds of verification, the account will be added to your

Your emails
When you tap on an email it will be displayed full screen, whereby you can file, delete or reply

All inboxes
If you have multiple accounts then tap on 'All Mailboxes' to view all of your emails from all of your accounts in one place

VIP
A recent addition to iPhone, users can now add certain senders to a VIP mailbox, to keep high-importance emails separate

Composing emails
Tap on this icon to start composing a new email. Your address will show up in accordance with the account you are using

To remove people from your VIP list, tap on the sender and then choose 'Remove from VIP'

active inboxes within the Mail app. Within the Mail app, you can tap on an individual mailbox to view only the emails relevant to that account, or you can tap on All Inboxes to view all of your received emails in one handy stream.

VIP Mailboxes

With the launch of iOS 6, Apple has redesigned Mail with a more streamlined interface for easier reading and writing. One of the new features is VIP Mailboxes. You can now set up a VIP list so that you'll never miss an important email – whether it's from your boss, your best friend or your accountant. To mark a person as a VIP, all you have to do it tap on their email address in a received message and then, on the Sender screen, select the 'Add to VIP' option. A star will then appear next to that person's email address to confirm that they have been marked as a VIP. This star will also be present next to all emails received from that person in your inbox. You can also find VIP emails quickly thanks to your new VIP inbox – just tap on this mailbox and all of the emails from all of your VIPs will be stored there for easy reference. So now you don't have to search your entire inbox for an important message, just go to your VIP mailbox.

Mark a person as a VIP

1 Highlight sender
From your inbox, open an email and then tap on the sender.

2 Place a star
Tap 'Add to VIP' and all emails from that person will go to your VIP inbox.

Mark or flag messages

1 Go to inbox
While in a mailbox, highlight a message in the list to the left.

2 Tap Edit
Tap the Edit button in the top-left corner of the column.

3 Tap to tick
Place a tick next to the message and then tap Mark.

4 Choose option
You can now choose to Flag or Mark as Read or Unread.

Calendar

You'll never miss an important event again with the iPhone's built-in date-keeper

You'll use it to...

Schedule events
Create new events for yourself and others

Plan ahead
View calendars by day, week, month or year

Sync with other devices
Get key dates from your other desktop calendars imported

Manage calendars
Activate or disable individual calendars

Get alerts
Set reminders for key events

Add birthdays
Import birthdays and anniversaries from your Contacts app

Fig 1 (above) With the Calendar app you can schedule events and appointments far into the future

Fig 2 (right) Press and hold on a time segment to bring up a box that lets you add numerous details to your event

Keep up to date in Calendar

Your iPhone's Calendar app is an intuitive way to keep up to date with events for the day, week, month or indeed the next 50+ years, and scheduling event dates into the app is as easy as selecting a calendar view and tapping on a time segment (Fig 1).

Schedule appointments

Making appointments is a quick and easy process in the Calendar app. Use the tabs at the bottom of the interface to select the 'Day' view and you will see the current day broken down into hourly time segments. To choose a future day, tap on the day in the monthly calendar to the left and a breakdown of the day will be presented down the screen. You can swipe up or down to scroll through the selected day and then to start scheduling an appointment by pressing and holding on the desired time segment. A New Event banner will then appear on the time segment, quickly followed by an Add Event box (Fig 2). Here you can enter a title and location for your appointment or event and then factor in the start and end times. Using the other options in this box, you can then choose

to repeat the event, invite people from your contacts, trigger alert reminders, add it to a particular calendar and add notes. Tap the Done button when all of the information has been added.

Changeable views

When you launch the app you will see a variety of different views, accessible by tabs at the bottom of the interface. By default the view is set to Day, with the current day broken down into one-hour segments, but you can easily tap on a different tab to view the calendar by Week, Month, Year or List. In Month view you don't see the timing of each scheduled event, but you can easily spot your busiest days. The List view displays your daily calendar with a list of all commitments for the month listed by day as you scroll down. If you have all of your calendars listed as shown, this section can essentially become a to-do list for you, and therefore a very useful piece of productivity on your iPhone.

Multiple calendars

One of the best things about the Calendar app is its versatility in allowing you to create different calendars for different areas of your life – such as personal and work – which you can then merge into one main calendar or deactivate them at will via the Calendars menu. You can create new calendars in the desktop Calendar app on your Mac (by clicking the File menu and choosing New Calendar). Any new calendars that you create can then be synced to your iPhone Calendar app via iCloud. This should happen automatically but you can speed up the process by tapping the sync button at the top of the Calendars menu.

You can also start scheduling new events by tapping the '+' button in the top corner

1 Find the date
Use the view tabs to find the date you wish to schedule on.

2 Scroll to time
Swipe up or down through the Day view to find the start time.

3 Press and hold
Add details into the Add Event box that appears.

4 Enter details
Enter locations and start and end times and then hit 'Done'.

Calendar

Sync birthdays and anniversaries

As you would expect from a built-in iOS app, Calendars works in perfect unison with other apps to make your life easier. In this instance, Calendar works with your Contacts app to display birthdays and anniversary dates that you have assigned to specific people within your Contacts database.

Ensure that you have birthdays assigned to people in your Contacts database and then, in your Calendar app, tap on the Calendars button in the top-left corner of the interface. Scroll down to the 'Other' section, where you will see Birthdays and then ensure that this option is selected (Fig 3). All birthdays and anniversaries assigned in your Contacts app will now be displayed as all-day events on the corresponding day in your calendar. To assign birthdays and anniversaries to specific people on Contacts, tap on a

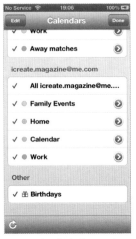

Fig 3 Tap on the Calendars button and ensure that the Birthdays calendar is activated in the list

Add an event
Tap the '+' icon to add a new event to your calendar. Once you've filled in the details, it will appear on the main screen

Your calendars
Tap on the Calendars button to view all of your active calendars and those that you subscribe to. You can manage your calendars from here

Events
A breakdown of the day shows all scheduled events. Tap on an event to view or edit the details

Calendar views
The row of tabs at the bottom of the interface will allow you to view calendars by Day, Week, Month, Year and List. Tap on a tab to change the view

You can also add events to a calendar by importing a calendar (.ics) file from an email

contact and then choose Edit. Scroll down to 'Add Field' and tap '+', then scroll down and choose to add either a Birthday or Date before factoring in the dates concerned.

Manage multiple calendars

Through the Calendar app you can subscribe to any calendar that uses the iCalendar (.ics) format. Many calendar-based services support calendar subscriptions, including iCloud, Yahoo! and Google, it's just a case of hunting around for the right ones.

To subscribe to a calendar, go to your Settings app and then choose the Mail, Contacts, Calendars option. Under Accounts, tap 'Add Account…' and then choose 'Other'. From here you can select the 'Add Subscribed Calendar' option.

You can also subscribe to iCal (or other .ics) calendars published on the web by tapping on a link to the calendar. As we have mentioned, you can also create new calendars in your Mac desktop calendar app and then sync them to your iPhone via iCloud. To manage your calendars, tap the Calendars button in the top-left corner of the interface and a list will display all available calendars that you can then enable or disable at will.

Subscribe to new calendars online

1 Find calendar
Search for iCal calendars online and then hit the Subscribe button.

2 Activate new calendar
The calendar will be added and can then be activated from the list.

Set event alerts

1 Tap on event
Tap on an existing event or create a new one by pressing '+'.

2 Tap on Alert
Scroll down the event box and then tap on the Alert option.

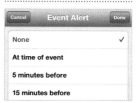

3 Select a time
From the list, select an option for when you want to be alerted.

4 Tap Done
Tap on 'Done' and your iPhone will automatically alert you.

Reminders

You need never forget to do something ever again with your iPhone's built-in memory bank

You'll use it to…

Make lists
Compose lists of tasks to complete

Set reminders
Get alerted when you need to complete particular tasks

Sync to iCloud
Get reminders pushed to other devices

Tick off tasks
A handy check-box lets you tick off items as you complete them

Check your calendar
Reminders syncs with the Calendar app to track your key dates

Never forget
An intuitive interface means reminding yourself is easy

Fig 1 (above) **With Reminders you can organise your life into simple 'to-do' lists**

Fig 2 (right) **Create a task and tap on it to bring up the Details box**

Set and schedule tasks

Reminders lets you organise your life, setting yourself tasks complete with due dates and lists (Fig 1). The app works with iCloud and your calendar accounts, so any changes that you make will update automatically on all of your iOS devices and computers. It's the simple way to never forget anything ever again!

Set a reminder

Setting yourself a new reminder is a quick and easy process and you can tap the '+' button to get started. You will now be prompted to enter a description of your task, so use the pop-up keyboard to summarise your task and then press the down arrow to make the keyboard disappear. You can then fine-tune the settings for the task by tapping on it in the list (Fig 2).

When the Details box appears, tap on the Remind Me button and then move the 'On a Day' slider to the On position. Now tap on the date and you will be able set it to any date and time you want. Once you have set the remind date, tap Done to return to the Details box and then select the Show More option. Here you can select a list for your reminder

to appear on and add any additional notes that you want. You can also set a priority for the task, and a suitable number of exclamation marks will appear next to the task depending on how urgent it has been deemed.

Create lists

Organising reminders into lists makes it easy to keep your work, personal and other to-dos separate from each other. The app comes with one list for active reminders, plus a built-in list of completed items – and you can also add other lists of your own. To create a list, tap on the 'List' tab at the top of the interface and then tap Edit. The option to Create New List will then appear under your various accounts, so tap on one and then type in the name of the list. There is also a scrolling calendar at the bottom of the screen to quickly jump to dates in order to add new reminders.

Reminders and iCloud

Reminders is just one of many apps that utilises Apple's iCloud service, which means that any lists and tasks that you create in the iCloud section will be synced and pushed to all of your other iOS devices and computers wirelessly.

It might not be possible to carry your iPhone around with your everywhere, so to get reminders created on iPhone pushed to your iPad would be useful. Go to Settings and ensure that the Reminders slider is turned on in the iCloud Settings to use this feature. In iOS 6, the ability to set location-based reminders was also added so that your device will chime in when you either leave or arrive at a certain address.

To delete lists, in List view, tap Edit and then hit the red '-' icon for each list you want to delete

Delete a reminder

1 Complete a task
Use your lists to help you remember to complete tasks.

2 Tick it off
When you complete a task, tap the small box to tick it off.

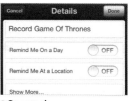

3 Open task
Tap on the task in question to bring up the Details box.

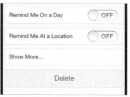

4 Delete task
Tap on the Delete button to remove it from the list.

Passbook

Passbook

Passbook is your digital wallet – find out how to make the most of it here…

You'll use it to…

Store cinema tickets
Bypass the box-office queue with tickets sent straight to your iPhone

Buy a coffee
Check your Starbucks card's balance

Save your boarding pass
Keep all your airline information together for simplified check-ins

Collect discount vouchers
Vouchers are issued to your Passbook

View loyalty cards
No more scrambling through your pocket for storecards

Check in to a hotel
All your reservation information is sent to your iPhone for safe keeping

Fig 1 (above) Though initially more popular in the US, Passbook is rapidly gaining ground in the UK

Fig 2 (right) You don't necessarily need to have downloaded a Passbook-compatible app to take advantage of its services

Using Passbook

Introduced with iOS 6, Passbook is a digital wallet that helps you keep track of all those day-to-day items such as discount coupons and cinema tickets (Fig 1) so they're all there with you whenever you need them.

Setting up Passbook

When you first launch Passbook, you'll be greeted by an introductory screen that includes a direct link to all Passbook-compatible apps in the App Store. Tap the link and download whichever apps you're most likely to use – the Starbucks app, for instance, was one of the first to be integrated into Passbook (Fig 2). Once you've downloaded a Passbook-compatible app, you'll need to register your details – sometimes within the app itself, sometimes on the company's website – including details of your preferred payment method. Sometimes, however, you don't need to have an app installed to take advantage of Passbook: Harvester Inns, for example, recently ran a promotion aimed only at Passbook users that involved clicking a link on the mobile version of its website that

generated a discount voucher if the user was running Safari for iOS 6. Virgin Atlantic also support Passbook – when you book online via the Virgin Atlantic website, you'll be asked if you want to save your boarding pass to your iOS device. To keep up to date with Passbook-compatible apps, check regularly at **http://www.itunes. com/passbookapps**.

Using your location

In order to be as helpful to you as possible, Passbook needs to take advantage of location services – the location-fixing feature powered by the GPS chip within your iOS device, plus Wi-Fi and network mast data. This way, your boarding pass can be ready and waiting for you when you reach the airport, or your cinema ticket can be ready to present on the door of your multiplex. To enable location services, go to Settings> Privacy>Location Services and make sure they're turned on.

Change Passbook's settings

As with all iOS apps, you can fine-tune Passbook to meet your own requirements. There are times, for instance, when you might not want a Passbook pass appearing on the lock screen of your iPhone, thereby giving away your personal details. To prevent this happening, go to Settings>General>Passcode Lock and turn Passcode on: you'll be prompted to create a passcode, if you haven't already. Go to Allow Access When Locked, and toggle Passbook off. To set up Passbook's notification options, go to Settings> Notifications>Passbook.

Finally, to share Passbook passes between your iOS devices, go to Settings>iCloud and make sure Passbook is turned on.

Passbook passes update themselves. To refresh, tap i, pull the pass downward and release it

1 Open Passbook To keep Passbook tidy by deleting old vouchers, first open Passbook.

2 Find your voucher Locate the voucher you want to delete and tap i (bottom right).

3 Deleting Now, tap the Trash can icon, located in the top-left corner of the voucher.

4 Deleted When asked to confirm the deletion, tap Delete, and the voucher is gone.

Notes

Use Notes to jot down your thoughts, new ideas or to act as a reminder for useful information

Take notes with ease

The Notes app is the perfect way to quickly write down those ideas, lists and anything else that pops into your head that you may need to remember later on. The Notes app also gives you all sorts of options for moving your notes to different locations and platforms, so you'll never forget anything ever again.

Write and share notes

You can create a new note by tapping the + icon in the top-right corner of the screen and all of your notes are automatically stored. Every note you create will be presented in an easily accessible list and anything you write down in the Notes app is simple to share with others from within the app itself.

To start sharing your notes, tap the Sharing icon that's located at the bottom of the screen (indicated by an arrow in a box, Fig 2) and you will be presented with options to Email, Message, Copy or Print. If you opt to Email your note, the contents of the current note will be copied and pasted into an email. All you have to do then is add the recipient's address in the correct field and you can mail it straight

Fig 1 (above) Notes provides plenty of screen space for you to write down and store a whole range of information

Fig 2 (right) You can easily share your Notes in a variety of different ways

out from within the Notes app. There's no need to cut, paste and switch between the apps yourself. You can print your notes wirelessly, and Notes is also iCloud compatible. Any notes you create can be accessed on all iOS devices.

Keyboard tricks

There are plenty of tricks and shortcuts that you can also use to your advantage. Pressing the space bar twice in quick succession will place a full stop and a space at the end of your sentence. Also, press and hold on the numbers key and quickly slide your finger to the number or symbol you wish to place before taking your finger off – it will switch back to the letters keyboard, allowing you to continue typing. To get a quick apostrophe, tap and hold the 'l' button and slide your finger upwards. These shortcuts are designed to make the Notes app an ideal place for quickly jotting down the key parts of your day even when you're in a rush, without having to worry about missing any of the key details along the way.

Notes and iCloud

Notes can be linked to iCloud. This gives you the ability to access your notes via different platforms such as a MacBook, iPad and iMac as well as your iPhone. If you use a **me.com** or **mac.com** email address for iCloud, go to the Settings and tap on iCloud and turn on Notes. If you use a Gmail or other web email account for iCloud, go to the Settings app and tap on the Mail option then tap Contacts and Calendars. Then turn on Notes for the account. All of these features enhance your Notes experience and make note-taking as simple as possible.

Enable Caps Lock in the Settings app and then activate it by double-tapping the Shift key

Change the Notes font

1 Settings Tap Settings on the main screen, then scroll down to the Notes section.

2 General Tap the Notes button and a new window will appear on the screen.

3 Font Note the three fonts listed at the top of the screen. Tap on the font you wish to use.

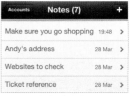

4 Return Go back to the Notes screen and notice that the new font has changed.

Maps

Use the Maps app to search for and find directions
to a location in both graphical or textual form

Fig 1 (above) **If you want to jump between global points, it's easy to rotate the Earth over multiple axes**

Fig 2 (right) **The items located in your search are highlighted by red pins**

Find your way around the world

Maps on your iPhone provides you with a real-time map that
can offer turn-by-turn directions that are spoken by the iPhone.
Alongside this there are interactive 3D views plus an amazing
Flyover feature. The entire world is open for examination (Fig 1) and
you can use the spread gesture to zoom in too, for even more detail.

Navigating

To navigate around the Maps app, all you have to do is tap the
search field and then type an address to go to your desired location.

You can also go to a
location at the same time as
inserting other information,
such as an intersection in
the USA (8th and Market)
or an area in London
(Westminster) or a landmark
in Australia (Sydney Opera
House). You can even enter a
postcode and business type
that is close to your current
location such as 'movies' or
'restaurants near me' (Fig 2).

You will also notice that, as
you enter the search field, a
long list of other suggestions
will appear in a drop-down
box, connected with your
search text. You can tap on
those too.

To navigate the actual
maps, you can move up

or down, left or right, drag the screen or rotate the map using two fingers on the screen. You will find a compass appearing in the upper-right corner to show the map's orientation. You can then return to the north-facing orientation by tapping on the compass icon again.

Bookmark a place

1 Route Select your start and end point and then tap on Route to see a visual representation.

Get directions

Once you have found your required location, press on the pin to reveal the banner. Then tap the arrow to open the full location description. Scroll down to find to 'Directions To Here' option. A new window will reveal your chosen location and three modes of transport: walking, car and bus.

Once you have selected how you want to travel, press the Route button on the top right-hand side of the window and a visual route will appear on the map. In a lot of cases, Maps will give you several route options, with Route 1 typically being the fastest and most direct.

2 End point Press on your final location to reveal a banner. This will feature the name.

3 Information Press the banner to see further information about the location. A window appears.

Turn-by-turn navigation

You need cellular data to make the most of this feature. Tap the Directions button on the top-left of the screen and then tap the mode of transport that you wish to use. Enter the start and end locations, then tap Route or choose a location or a route from the list. Maps follows your progress as you go and speaks turn-by-turn directions to guide you towards your destination. To show or hide the controls, tap the screen. You can view the turn-by-turn directions by tapping Start, then swiping on the instruction left to see the next instruction. Tap the Overview button to see the whole route on a single screen.

4 Bookmark At the base is the Add To Bookmarks button. Press here to save.

Press the Overview button on the top right-hand corner to get a view of the whole route

Maps

Flyover

With the Flyover feature in Maps, you can see a selection of major metro areas from the air with photorealistic, interactive 3D views (Fig 3). The feature is not available for the entire planetary surface, although more cities are constantly being added and updated.

The feature enables you to explore cities in high resolution via zoom, pan, tilt and rotate gestures. To use the Flyover you should zoom into your desired location until the Flyover mode becomes active. You can tell if Flyover mode is available because you will be able to tap the building button on the bottom-left of the screen.

Alternatively, you can drag two fingers up the screen to tilt the 3D building effect. This gesture command adjusts the camera angle. Use other gesture commands to navigate around the map.

Fig 3 The Flyover feature can produce some highly complex 3D objects

Search bar
On the top right-hand side is the search bar to search for any location in the world

Directions
Placed on the top left-hand corner, tap here to generate locations to and from a place

Location
The location is signified by the red pin which, when tapped, triggers a bar than can provide further information

Page corner
Under the bottom right-hand page corner lie the map type, print and Show Traffic options

After selecting your style, you can return to the map page by pressing on the screen

As you move around the map, depending on the complexity of the map surface and the number of buildings present, you may see some slight delays as the 3D objects are built on the grid surface by the iPhone. We don't recommend using Flyover on a cellular data connection – it'll be slow to load and will eat into your data plan.

Standard, Hybrid, and Satellite map views

When you are viewing a map location, there are three main ways that this information can be presented to you. If you want to see the most realistic view on the location, then you should select the Satellite view. This produces a bird's-eye view point on the ground and is the most realistic of the three, showing true-to-life features such as major landmarks and landscapes plus rivers and roads.

On the other end of the scale is the Standard view, which provides you with a similar view as you might see on a paper map. This includes road names plus the names of areas and indications of landmarks such as parks, schools, shopping centres and much more. The Hybrid view utilises the satellite landscape but inserts the standard-view labelling to give you a blend that mixes the realistic with the informative that might be better suited to some.

Access the different map views

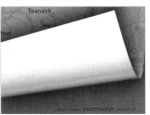

1 The corner Press the bottom-right-hand corner of the map to expose the map styles menu.

2 Change the style There are three map styles revealed under the map page. Choose one to use.

Share a location

1 Search location Select your start and end point and then tap on Route.

2 Information Press on your final location to reveal a banner. This will feature the name.

3 Find the button Examine the box – notice the Share Location button on the bottom left.

4 Share Location Press Share Location and select your method such as email, Facebook, etc.

Siri

Siri is a voice-command interface system, an intelligent personal assistant for your iPhone

You'll use it to...

Go hands free
Give voice commands to your iPhone

Speak naturally
Siri understands natural speech

Set functions
Set an alarm or similar utility by voice

Open apps
Ask Siri to open any app for you

Get directions
Find directions via the Maps app

Communicate socially
Post messages to Twitter and Facebook

Your personal assistant

With Siri, a voice-controlled interface that uses natural speech to initiate commands, you can write and send a message, schedule a meeting or place a FaceTime call. But that's not all, you can also get directions, set a reminder and search the web (although it's not available for the iPhone 4 or below).

Search the web with Siri

To start Siri, enter the Settings section and tap on General. Then tap on Siri to enter the Siri-specific settings. Swipe the switch to the On position. Siri is now enabled.

To activate the Siri interface, press the Home button until Siri appears on the screen. You'll hear two beeps and see the "What can I help you with?" text appear on the screen. Give the Siri interface your web search command using speech (Fig 2). The microphone icon will light up. Talking with Siri can be continued by tapping on the microphone icon. The interface then waits for you to stop speaking. If you have completed your command, tap the microphone icon to end. This action is recommended when there is background

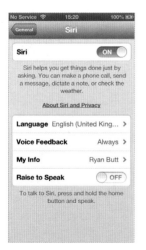

Fig 1 (above) You can enable the Siri interface by entering the Settings section

Fig 2 (right) Requesting a web page automatically loads the browser software and loads your requested page

noise to contend with, and It can also speed up your conversation with Siri.

After you have stopped talking, the Siri interface displays what it has heard and it will then respond to your query. You will be taken to your browser where your requested web page will load with your search results.

Send an email with Siri

1 Start Siri Press the Home key for a few seconds to open the Siri interface.

Get directions with Siri
Before you can get directions from Siri, you need to tap Settings and scroll down to the Privacy section. Tap Privacy to open the window on the right. The Location Services should be On. Look down to the Siri switch and turn that to the On position. Press the Home button until Siri appears, then give your direction instructions. The interface will then open the Maps app and provide you with a full set of visual and aural directions.

Siri is smooth enough to jump straight into the turn-by-turn directions, following and prompting you as you go.

Create family links
You can teach Siri about yourself by constantly using it. Siri learns and expands its database on you to make its operation easier and more efficient. Siri also obtains its infon from your personal info card (My Info) in the Contacts app. If you tap Settings>General>Siri>My Info then tap your name, Siri can learn from your family links, so put those relationships on your info card. If you tell Siri to text your sister, Siri asks you who your sister is and then adds that relationship to your personal info card. These shortcuts are great for when you're in a hurry and you want to quickly fire off a message to say that you're running late. Siri is the ultimate assistant in this sense.

2 Send email If you ask Siri to Send Email, it will respond with a recipient request.

3 Email content Tell Siri who you want to send it to and state its contents.

4 Send Tell Siri to send the email message to your contact. Siri will respond once completed.

Ask Siri a trivia question and it should have an answer for you, or know somewhere that does

Clock

Keep track of the time wherever you are in the world and never be late again with the Clock app

You'll use it to...

Browse world times
See the time in cities across the globe

Set an alarm
Have different alarms for numerous tasks

Measure elapsed time
Use the stopwatch and see time go by

Measure time intervals
See the time left between tasks

Catch the latest news
The clock links to Yahoo! in your location

Check the weather
View summaries of local climates

Keep track of time

As well as letting you see the time across the world (Fig 1), the Clock app also allows you to time the interval between events or use a stopwatch. It also operates as a brilliant alarm clock with the possibility of setting multiple alerts.

Set an alarm

When you tap the + icon in the top right-hand corner, you are able to begin setting an alarm (Fig 2). Use the dials to configure the exact time by scrolling up and down using your fingers until you find the right one. You can then decide whether or not you want to repeat the alarm, which you can do on any day of the week, and whether or not you would like to include a snooze function.

It is possible to label that particular alarm with any name you wish. For example, you could decide that you would like to label one 'Waking Up' and another one for a Meeting.

It is also possible to add a particular sound to your alarm. When you have completed this, the alarm will show on the calendar within the Clock app so that you can see, at a glance,

Fig 1 (above) You can add pages and pages of world times – just tap Add

Fig 2 (right) Tap the + icon in order to begin setting up your alarms for various tasks

when any of your alarms have been set. It is possible to edit any of these by selecting Edit in the top left-hand corner. You can then use the toggle bar next to each alarm to turn individual ones on and off as you need them.

Stopwatch and timers

When you tap on the Stopwatch tab at the bottom of the screen, you are able to begin measuring elapsed time. Likewise, when you select Timer, you can measure time intervals.

With the Stopwatch, you simply tap Start and the time will begin to increase. When you tap Stop, it will cease. The Stopwatch has a great lap timer, too. Tapping Lap when a lap is finished will show the time that the lap took to complete.

On the Timer, you simply need to input the timescale you want using the dials and then tap Start. The countdown will then begin. You can even set the alarm that will sound when the countdown reaches zero.

World clocks

As well as being able to see a set of five default time zones of Cupertino, New York, Paris, Beijing and Tokyo, tapping Add lets you find any location around the world and see the exact time at that particular location too.

When you tap the Add button, you will be shown a list of included time zones. You can either scroll through these and find one that you want, or you can decide instead to use the keyboard and input a search term. Tap the result you are looking for and the clock will be added to those that already exist. The time will also be placed on the world map.

You can quickly turn off your alarms by going to Alarm and moving the slider to the Off position

Add music to an alarm

1 Add alarm Tap on the + button to Add Alarm and then you need to select Sound.

2 Select song Under the category of Songs, some tunes will be listed

3 Pick a song Either tap one of these options or alternatively select Pick a song.

4 Search for tunes When you have found the one you want to use, tap it to choose.

FaceTime

FaceTime

FaceTime is ideal for talking to your friends, family or colleagues in real-time via video link

You'll use it to…

Make video calls
Talk face to face with friends and family

Talk to other devices
Call from iPhone to iPad or MacBook

Switch cameras
Easily switch from front to rear cameras

Call for free
FaceTime calls are free of charge

Use FaceTime on TV
Great for making group calls

Add Favourites
Create FaceTime favourites

Fig 1 (above) FaceTime gives you an easy way to chat with friends and family

Fig 2 (right) Make sure FaceTime is turned on in the Settings app first

Chat face-to-face

FaceTime allows you to undertake video calls with another user of a compatible Apple device: iPad, iPod touch, MacBook and iMac. The app also includes a picture-in-picture facility while you're talking (Fig 1), so that can see how you look to the person on your screen.

Call a contact with FaceTime

To enable you to use FaceTime, you will initially need to set up an Apple ID, if you haven't already obtained one. You'll also need a Wi-Fi connection or cellular 3G link that can connect you to the Internet for the app to work.

When you open FaceTime, you may be prompted to sign in using your Apple ID or to create a new account. Before you can make your FaceTime call, tap the Contacts app and find the details you require. Then choose a name and either tap that person's phone number or their email address, either will do to open FaceTime.

When making the call, you can move the iPhone in either landscape or portrait orientation. It is advisable, however, to lock the rotation before you make your call to avoid disturbing orientation changes during your chat.

If you have recently called a FaceTime contact, you can call them again quickly by visiting the Recents section found within the Phone app. You will see a small video-camera icon placed next to the contact.

Add favourites
Using the FaceTime app is similar, in practice, to using the Phone app. You can make calls, interact with callers, respond to the Recent list of missed calls and so on.

In a similar way, FaceTime will also require, at some point, time-saving additions that will speed up the process. Saving your contacts to a Favourites section, for example, may prove to be useful. To add a favourite, go to a contact in your list, select them, and then tap the Add To Favourites option. You will then be asked if you would like this favourite to be a voice call or FaceTime favourite. A star icon will appear against their name in the contacts list from now on, and you'll also find them under the Favourites shortcut, at the bottom of the screen in your Contacts app.

Chat on multiple devices
One of the more useful features of the FaceTime app is its ability to be used in between devices. Not just devices of the same type, either. While you can easily utilise FaceTime between iPhone and iPhone, you can also use it between an iPad and iPhone, iPhone and iMac and iPhone and MacBook.

There are slight differences in how communication is initiated, however. The requirement of an Apple ID is constant but, in addition, you will need a phone number if you want to call an iPhone. To call an iPad, iPod touch or Mac, you can use an email.

To FaceTime a Favourite from the list, simply tap on the name in the Contacts app

1 **Picture in picture** Look at the small image of yourself to see what your caller can see.

2 **Switch cameras** Toggle the camera so that your caller can see what you are seeing.

3 **Mute** Press the icon at the bottom of the screen. The other person will not hear your words.

4 **End call** To end the call, press the End button, positioned at the bottom of the screen.

FaceTime

Fig 3 Troubleshooting can largely be completed in the FaceTime settings screen

Troubleshooting

If FaceTime is not working as it should, then tap on the Settings icon and scroll down the headings until you reach the FaceTime header. Tap on the button and a set of FaceTime settings will then appear (Fig 3).

Firstly, make sure that the FaceTime app is switched On. To do this, swipe the button to the right to the On position. Make sure that you have a valid Apple ID, which will be displayed at the top of this screen. Re-enter your Apple ID if it is incorrect.

If you are out of range of your Wi-Fi router, you will need to depend on 3G in order to make FaceTime calls. Make sure that you are using 3G if you wish to utilise Cellular data, and to use, swipe the Use Cellular Date switch to the right so that it displays the On

Favourites
Tap this tab to see your FaceTime Favourites

Search
If you've got a lot of Contacts, you may find the search function very handy indeed!

Easy scrolling
Drag your finger down this alphabet to quickly scroll down your list – it's useful if your contact list is large!

Add contact
Press the + button to add a contact to your list – you can then enter more information

To remove a FaceTime email contact, press the blue arrow and hit Remove This Email

position. If you turn this switch to the Off position, it will look for a Wi-Fi connection. Also make sure that you are using a valid Caller ID and contact details.

FaceTime on TV

One of the great things about FaceTime is that you can talk in real-time with a friend or colleague for free while using high-quality images and sound. The downside, however, is that the entire experience is very one-on-one. You might be able to squeeze one extra face on your iPhone, but it's not the most comfortable manner of trying to communicate on a group level.

Of course, with more than two individuals involved in a conversation, the best solution would be to use a much larger screen. For many, the best screen to use of its type would be a TV. Fortunately, that's not a problem for FaceTime and the iPhone, which can utilise a 30-pin/lightning to VGA adaptor to enable FaceTime to be displayed on your own TV. As long as you keep the iPhone positioned so that the camera points at you and gets everyone in the frame, then such a variation is an ideal method for having large group or family conversations.

Turn FaceTime on

1 Settings Go to the Settings app, then scroll down until you see the FaceTime option.

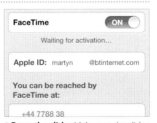

2 Press the slider Make sure the slider is turned to on, and then start adding some contacts!

Apps during FaceTime

1 Launch FaceTime Find your Contact and make your call. Connect with the other user.

2 Home button To use an app during a FaceTime call, press the Home button on the iPhone.

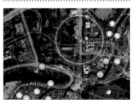

3 Select app On the iPhone, select the required app and then press it to open.

4 Return to FaceTime To return to the call, press the green bar at the top of the screen.

Camera

Camera

With the iPhone's built-in camera, you have the power to take both photos and video at your fingertips

You'll use it to…

Take photos
Ideal when you're on the move

Take a video
Monitor the video on your screen

Use location services
Tagged images can be used by apps

Take a self-portrait
Take an image of yourself

View images
Examine your photos while on the move

View videos
You can also view your suite of videos

Take photos on the go

If you own an iPhone, you can take still photos with the built-in camera. You are also able to record videos either the front or rear-facing camera. Both lenses can be also used to point at your face for use with FaceTime.

Shoot photos

To take a photo with the iPhone you must first open up the Camera app. Then make sure that the Camera/Video switch, situated at the bottom right-hand side of the screen, is set to the Camera mode. To do this, move the switch to the camera icon position.

The next stage is to lift the iPhone and aim it at your chosen subject. Make sure that you frame your subject as you want it to appear in the shot, then pause a second. This allows the iPhone to focus properly (a rectangle briefly appears where the camera is focusing and setting the exposure).

When you photograph people, iPhone uses face detection to automatically focus on and balance the exposure across up to ten

Fig 1 (above) When taking a photo or recording a video, frame your subject within the screen first

Fig 2 (right) Make sure that the camera icon is selected to take a single image

faces. Tap on the Camera icon that is situated within the screen, half-way up on the right-hand side in landscape mode. When you press, the image will be taken and a shutter sound-effect will be triggered to indicate that an image has been snapped. In addition you'll see an iris animation move across the screen which provides a visual indication that your photograph has been taken.

Take faster and better photographs

Rather than having to press a virtual shutter button every time you want a shot, you can also use the volume buttons when taking photos. It works exactly the same way as the capture icon on the screen, but means you can hold the iPhone steady. It is close to the lens, however, so be careful not to place your finger in the wrong position. Also, turn on Grid Lines from the Options to compose correctly. The iPhone 5 also comes with a built-in panorama feature that guilds you through the process of taking a series of photos that your iPhone will then stitch together to make a single image.

2 Options Press the Options button in the middle of the top row.

Share your images

With a little practice, you can take some great images with your iPhone. If you want to show these off, you can easily share your stored images with a variety of friends, family and colleagues via email, text message or even a Tweet.

To do this, choose a photo that you wish to send and tap it. A new set of controls will appear. Press the Share icon from the tab at the bottom of the screen. This will reveal a range of icons that will allow you to share your images. Press one of them to activate the app and initiate the share.

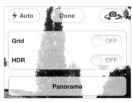

3 Swipe When the Grid menu appears, swipe the button to the On position.

Within the share menu, you can also select the Copy icon to copy your image for use elsewhere

4 Arrange image Use the on-screen grid to compose and arrange your image.

Camera

Shoot videos

To take a video with your iPhone, first open up the Camera app. Then make sure that the Camera/Video switch situated at the bottom right-hand side of the screen is set to the Video mode. When you change the mode from camera to video, the iPhone confirms the action by triggering an iris animation which then recedes to reveal a new start icon. Instead of the camera button, this icon is now a simple red dot button.

Lift the iPhone and aim it at your chosen subject. Tap on the new red icon that is situated at the bottom of the screen, in the centre. When you press this button on the iPhone, a sound effect will be triggered to indicate the start of the video. When the video is running, a timer will note the passing seconds, in the bottom left-

Lens
Press here to jump between the front and rear-facing camera lenses

Flash
Use this icon to turn the flash on or off, or set it to automatic

Options
This allows you to turn on the grid as well as HDR settings, or start a panorama

Bottom Window
The window at the bottom of the screen shows you the last photo you took

In the Edit screen, next to the frame viewer, press the play icon to run the video and view your work

hand part of the screen. To stop recording your video, press the red button icon again. The saved video will then be placed as a small icon on the bottom left-hand corner. Press this to play back your saved movie sequence.

Edit and trim videos

When you have recorded your videos, you can then edit them by trimming the frames from the beginning and also from the end of a video or from any other video in your Camera Roll album. You can also replace the original video that you have recorded or you can save the newly edited video as a video clip.

To trim your video, play the video to be edited and tap the screen. You'll see a set of controls. At the top of the screen, a frame viewer will appear, exposing all of the individual frames of your video. To trim your video, press and drag one end of the video, then press the yellow Trim button. Once you have done this, a short menu will drop down and ask you if you want to Trim Original or Save A New Clip. If you select the Trim Original option, then the trimmed frames from your sequence will be permanently deleted from the original video.

Save clip

1 Yellow trim To save your video as a new video clip, press the yellow Trim button.

2 Camera Roll Press Save as New Clip. The clip with then be saved in your Camera Roll album.

Share on YouTube

1 Create video Load the Camera app, then start and save your desired video.

2 Menu Press the video screen to allow menu options to pop-up on the screen.

3 Forward Press the Share icon which is found in the bottom left-hand side of the screen.

4 YouTube transfer Press the YouTube icon. Type in your details to send the video.

Photos

Use this app to keep your precious photos in perfect order and browse them with ease

You'll use it to…

View your images
See photographs in stunning clarity

Zoom in on pictures
Use your fingers to get extra detail

See thumbnails
View images at a glance

Share photographs
Send images via social media or mail

Print images
Create a hard copy of any photo

Produce a slideshow
Have images automatically display

View your images

Images which you take via screenshots, from the web or using the built-in camera, automatically appear within the Photos app. These are then available to you within one handy place, allowing you to scroll through them and see thumbnails for easy access.

The Camera Roll

When you take a photograph using your iPhone's camera, it will appear in your Camera Roll, a section in the Photos app on the iPhone. It is also possible to see the Camera Roll by opening the Camera app and tapping the icon in the bottom left-hand corner.

If you want to view an image in your Camera Roll, you can do this one of two ways: either go direct to Photos by tapping on the app on the home screen or view your shots via the Camera app. Then tap on one of the images to instantly bring it up on the entire screen and flick left and right to go through them.

When viewing a photo or video in the Camera Roll album, you can also tap the screen to bring up some controls. This will allow you to edit, share or even delete

Fig 1 (above) All of your images are displayed as thumbnails so you can jump to any photo quickly and easily

Fig 2 (right) You can make photographs appear in the full iPhone screen by tapping a thumbnail in the Camera Roll

an image. You can also go back to your Camera Roll to view the thumbnails again for quick selection. You can also view a slideshow of all you photos by tapping the Play icon in the menu bar.

AirPlay
You can view photographs from the iPhone on an Apple TV, a low-priced set-top box for your television. This is done via AirPlay which is built in to your iOS device. Both your iOS and Apple TV devices need to be on the same Wi-Fi network. You then open Photos and locate and tap the AirPlay icon before selecting your Apple TV from the list. You can then begin playback.

Photo Stream
The Photo Stream pulls in photographs from a variety of sources. You are even able to take a photo on another device, such as an iPad, and have it appear on your iPhone via iCloud. The Photo Stream is also the place where imported photos from a digital camera will go. You can also sync with iPhoto on a Mac.

Indeed, iCloud is a brilliant manager of your Photo Stream and your last 1,000 photos are held. When you want to touch up photos or keep them, they just need to be saved to the Camera Roll.

Slideshows
When you take photographs, it is with the intention of viewing them later on to relive the memories for yourself, or show them off to friends and family. While you can open individual photos one by one and show people, you can also create a slideshow. This will play automatically, so people can view them without intervention. It is possible to customise your slideshow and really make it your own

Send an image to Photo Stream by tapping it and selecting Share, then choose Photo Stream

Create a new album

1 **Tap Plus** When in Photos, tap the Plus tab at the top of the screen.

2 **Add Album** In the top left-hand corner of the screen, look for the + icon, then tap it.

3 **Enter name** After entering the name of an album, press Save and choose some images.

4 **Adding photos** Press Done and these photos will then appear within the new album.

Photos

by adding transitions and background music. All you have to do is open up the Photos app and tap the Play icon on a photo. you're viewing. You can select to turn Music on and find a piece to play from the music that is stored on your device. You can also choose your preferred slide transitions, ranging from visual dissolves to origami effects. These will give your slideshow an interesting and more polished feel.

When you have finished, simply tap Start Slideshow and it will begin to play all of the photos in your Camera Roll from the start. You can open specific albums and play images from there if you want a more targeted slideshow. This is great for showcasing your holiday snaps, for instance.

Fig 3 The slideshows allow for music and snazzy visual transitions

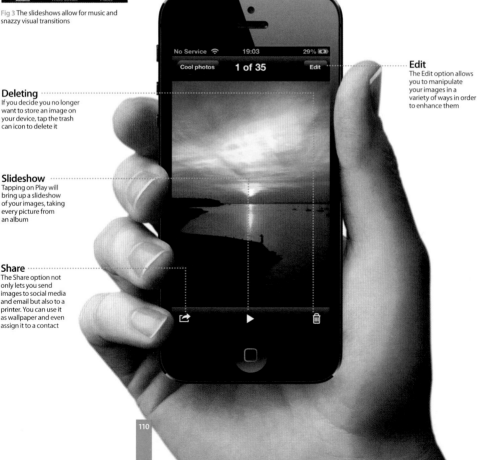

Edit
The Edit option allows you to manipulate your images in a variety of ways in order to enhance them

Deleting
If you decide you no longer want to store an image on your device, tap the trash can icon to delete it

Slideshow
Tapping on Play will bring up a slideshow of your images, taking every picture from an album

Share
The Share option not only lets you send images to social media and email but also to a printer. You can use it as wallpaper and even assign it to a contact

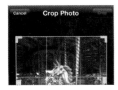

Use the built-in grid guidelines when you are cropping to centre your photograph perfectly

Edit your photos

Are your shots looking a little shabby? Do they need a bit of a lift? You can easily make simple and subtle enhancements from within your Photos app to really make your favourite images shine.

To get started with your editing, open up a photograph and tap Edit at the top of the screen. This will then take you to the editing mode, which offers you simple-yet-effective techniques to enhance your images. The features available range from rotation to enhance, red-eye removal and crop.

Pressing rotate will flip your image by 90 degrees. Keep tapping to rotate it back to the original image. The enhance option automatically scans your photo and then adds an effect which gives it greater depth and colour. For example, a washed-out image can be made more vivid. Red-eye reduction asks you to tap each eye. It will then remove any redness from it. And finally, Crop places a series of lines across your image and allows you to trim away the excess for a perfectly composed capture.

By using these techniques, you will be able to make some small alterations to your photographs that can make a big difference to their appearance. Images are then saved to your Camera Roll.

Make photos instantly better

1 Find an image Locate and select a photograph that you would like to apply edits to.

2 Tap Enhance Tapping Enhance will give your photo an automatic lift, for pleasing results.

Use the Shared Photo Streams feature

1 Find Photo Stream Tap the Photo Stream option (the centre tab at the bottom of the screen).

2 Add a stream Tap the + icon in the top-left of the screen to call up a window.

3 Fill in details In the To entry box, type the iCloud email of the person you are sharing with.

4 Create Tap Create and a new album appears. Open the album and tap Add Photos.

Game Center

Get social and allow others in on the action
when you're playing games on your iPhone

You'll use it to…

Compete against others
Invite people to join in your games

Expand your network
Be more social with multiplayer

Get going quickly
All you need is your Apple ID

Assign email addresses
Let people find you with ease

Always be connected
Sign in and you're in the game

Climb the leaderboards
See how your score ranks against friends

Fig 1 (above) The Game Center app is the place to go on your iPhone for multiplayer gaming and challenges

Fig 2 (right) Your profile will be the first you see after logging in

Play games with friends

The Game Center app is the hub of your gaming life on your iPhone. You can use it to invite others to join you in multiplayer games and you can also compare your score with other people to see how your skills rank against the best. There is an auto-matching facility too which lets you hook up with other gamers around the world.

Set up Game Center

As long as you are running iOS 4.1 or later, you will see the Game Center icon on your Home Screen. When you tap on this, the Game Center will open and it will ask you if it can send Push Notifications. This means it will inform you of any gaming details relevant to the titles you are playing. You can choose yes at this stage and, if you decide later you don't want it, just turn it off via the Settings app.

To log in to Games Center, input your Apple ID password when you are prompted (Fig 1), and tell the app where you reside and your date of birth. This information is intended to prevent under-age play of certain game titles which have age restrictions. Once you have entered this info, confirm the terms and

conditions, choose a Nickname to be identified by and you can also add another email if you like. For every email address that you add, you will be sent a message and asked to confirm the address via an internal link.

At this stage, you are in the Game Center and ready to go. All you have to do next is add a few gaming friends to play against.

Game Center friends

Select the Requests icon within the Game Center app. It will now allow you look for friends which you can do via their Nickname if you know it or you can also use their email address. The app lets you write a message to them as part of the invite and it's worth doing this so that your friend knows that it is really from you. Of course, you will not only be seeking friends. They will look for you too. Requests will appear in the app if they've approached by Nickname or via email if an email address is used. You can also scroll through your friends list and see what everyone you know has been playing recently, and what games they have in common with you.

Achievements

The Games page shows all of the games you have that are Game Center compatible. To access your Achievements, tap on a game. This will show what can be earned within each title and it will also have a description and a point value – the higher the number of points, the better you will look.

Achievements give you some bragging rights since you can compare your points with those of friends, creating a friendly and competitive spirit.

If you want to create a fresh Apple ID, this is easy to do on the app's opening page

Add a friend

1 Tap Friends When you are in the Game Center app, tap the Friends button.

2 Add friend Tap the + button in the top left. Input the user name of someone you know.

3 Use email You can also enter your friends' email addresses to find the right people.

4 Tap OK When a friend accepts an invitation, their name will appear on your friends list.

Game Center

Play online

When you are all set up and ready to play, simply go to the Game Center on your iPhone by tapping the icon. Once the app is open, you can do one of two things: play games against a friend or simply play on your own.

For the former option, tap on the Friends tab. Both you and your chosen gaming buddy will have to have downloaded the same game in order to play together. To see what you can play together, a list of games that you both have in common will appear under each Friend. All you have to do is tap the name of a game you want to play to send an invitation to your pal. This will let them know that you want to hook up. They will need to respond to this so you have to hang fire until they Accept or Decline your request.

Fig 3 By tapping on an achievement, you can send your friends a challenge

Leaderboards
The aim is to amass a load of points so that you can be the king of gaming and you can see where you fall on the leaderboard

Invite
When you are ready to invite friends to play, all you need to do is tap on the Friends icon in order to be taken to the various options

Status
You can change your photo and declare whether you are ready for action or not by tapping the bottom icon to the far left

Games
Games can be chosen by tapping on the Games icon. You will then be able to see the games that you have in common with your friends

114

Once you add friends to Game Center, their scores will appear in the left-hand column

When they accept it the game begins, so tap Play. You will now accumulate points. As we've said, you can also play alone, in which case you'll just tap the name of the game. When complete, tap Done to end.

Leaderboards

When you select a game, you will be able to see your ranking and achievements within that game, if they exist. You will also be able to see the leaderboards and these show stat tables for that day as well as for the week and an all-time tally. You can tap on the name of a player and this will show their statistics and where they lie in the gaming scheme of things.

Once you've found out who is the reigning champion of a particular game, you are able to send them a friend request by tapping on their name. You can also send them a challenge via the same pop-up window. Not all leaderboards are the same and they depend on the game that you have selected. The idea is generally the same though, and the leaderboards are a wonderful way to foster a competitive spirit and show the progress that you and your friends are making.

Finding leaderboards

1 View tables Tap Games, select a game title and then press the Leaderboard tab.

2 Different days You will now see the leaderboards for today, this week and all time.

Edit your status

1 It's Me Tap on the Me tab and you will see your account page with all your details.

2 Tap status In order to alter you gaming status, tap within the Status box.

3 Keyboard Use the keyboard to input your status and tap Done when finished.

4 Add photo While you're here, you may as well add a photo. Tap Add Photo to insert a pic.

Newsstand

Newsstand

Never darken the door of a newsagent again with magazines direct to your iPhone

You'll use it to…

Buy newspapers
Read through many national papers

Subscribe to magazines
Get a subscription to your favourite mag

Enjoy interactivity
Play with video and audio

Get free issues
Enjoy a trial issue of many publications

Rate publications
Tell publishers what you think

Navigate with ease
Flick through mags as you would a real one

Read thousands of magazines on the go

With Newsstand, you can enjoy subscriptions to your favourite magazines and newspapers and even have new issues automatically download to your iPhone. There are thousands of publications out there to suit all tastes and pockets, and there are sometimes freebies to be had, too.

The Newsstand Store

When you open the Newsstand app for the very first time, you will see a set of empty shelves. These will obviously need filling!

To do this, in the top right-hand corner, you will see the 'Store' button. Tap on this and you will be taken to the front end of Apple's Newsstand Store where you can see what is new and noteworthy, what's hot and a slider that shows you flagged-up content. Browsing around the Newsstand Store, you'll soon see that there is a lot to choose from. At the bottom of the screen, there are several options. You can see Featured, Top Charts, Genius and more. Tapping on these will take you to other parts of the App Store. To view more publications, tap on See All next to the various

Fig 1 (above) The Newsstand store front end gives you a great flavour of the publications on offer

Fig 2 (right) All Newsstand apps are listed here in a single columns, which you can then scroll through

categories on the right-hand side of the iPhone screen. This will then list all of the magazines or papers of interest to you in a single column. The thumbnail shows the front cover of the publication and tapping on one brings up a window for a closer look on what's on offer inside that particular publication.

Delete a magazine

1 Open Newsstand Tap on the Newsstand icon and the app will open.

Buy a magazine

In order to buy a magazine or paper from Newsstand, tap on the thumbnail of the publication you want and read the details as well as ratings and reviews before deciding if you wish to install it. If you do, tap Install and the app will download. The app will appear within Newsstand. To open the publication, tap on the thumbnail. Each app operates in its own way but there will be an opportunity to buy individual issues with most of them. Tap the price and the issue will download. From this individual publication menus, you can also get subscriptions as well as manage the issues you already have.

2 Tap and hold You will see magazines on a rack. Tap and hold on one of them.

Subscribe to a magazine

To subscribe, look for the subscription option in the magazine app. There may be different levels of subscription, so choose the most suitable. Once you've done this, you can ask the app to automatically push the magazines to your iPhone so you never miss an issue.

You are then able to launch new issues of magazines or papers in the Newsstand folder when they're delivered. The app will also alert you when new issues are available. To manage your subscriptions, go to Settings, then 'iTunes & App Stores'. Tap 'View Apple ID' and scroll down to 'Manage App Subscriptions'.

3 Shaking The icons will begin to shake. Tap the X next to one you wish to delete.

4 And delete! When asked if you want to delete a magazine and its data, tap Delete.

Some publications have free subscriptions so keep an eye out for these great-value papers and mags

Newsstand

Read and navigate your content

To read a magazine on your iPhone, tap View next to the issue you wish to look at and it will appear on your iPhone screen. Just by simply moving your fingers back and forth in a sliding motion, you are able to flick from one page to another just as you would with a paper-based publication.

By tapping the screen, you will typically see a range of options. These include the ability to search through a publication, show or add bookmarks and view the list of contents for easier navigation. There will also invariably be a Share option and Settings.

At the bottom of the screen, you will be able to see the pages as thumbnails and scroll through them (Fig 3). By tapping on a page, it will open and this is a great way of flicking straight through to a

Fig 3 You will be able to search inside a magazine using the search facility

Navigating
Tapping this button will take you back to the previous screen, useful if you want to return to a specific menu

Information
When you tap on the title of a publication, you will see an information box which gives you extra details, ratings and reviews and related info

Tabs
Select one of the bottom tabs to view the most popular magazines, features mags and more

Download
Select the Install or Free button to download the magazine app. You'll then be able to purchase individual issues or subscribe

Tilt the iPhone on its side and, in many cases, you can view extra magazine features in widescreen

section without having to keep swiping left and right to find it. If you need to see more detail on a page then simply use two fingers to pinch and pull. This will zoom in and out.

Interactive magazines

Interactive magazines go much further than the simple recreations of a printed page on an iPhone. They add extra multimedia content to a magazine, whether it be a video embedded on to a page which can be called up with a tap or an animated infographic in which the component parts come to life when you tap or manipulate them. It brings a whole new dimension to a magazine and really showcases the ability of publications on an iPhone.

Having audio included with your favourite magazine, for example, can allow you to listen to snippets of an interview as well as read about the subject matter. The beauty of this feature is that such publications are continuing to evolve and take advantage of the possibilities of an iPhone. Even if it is something as simple as links to other websites, that is classed as an interactive magazine. This greatly enhances your magazine experience and enables you to get much more for your subscription money.

Using interactive content

1 Playing videos Simply tap on a video within an interactive mag and the content comes alive.

2 All sorts It's not uncommon for publications to include interactive content - like live social feeds.

Turn automatic downloads on/off

1 Go to the Settings Navigate to the Settings app and choose 'iTunes and App Stores'.

2 Tap Apple ID Tap on your Apple ID, which you will see at the top of the screen.

3 Input password You will be asked to input your Apple ID password, so type this in now.

4 Turn it off Go to Newsstand and manage your automatic downloads.

iBooks

Enjoy a good read without having to trek to the library, and save some trees at the same time

You'll use it to...

Buy books
Access the iBooks Store

Read fiction
Flick through thousands of novels

Scour textbooks
Become more educated

Save your PDFs
Place PDFs in iBooks

Search through books
Find specific terms in books

Enlarge text
Make books comfortable to read

Fig 1 (above) Take your book library with you wherever you go

Fig 2 (right) The iBookstore is packed with all kinds of books and you will be spoiled for choice

Read books on your iPhone

Using iBooks, you can not only browse books and buy them in the iBookstore, you can also read them on your iPhone and take advantage of great search facilities. The app puts an entire library of books at your fingertips.

The iBookstore

The iBookstore is the place to go to choose from thousands of books to buy and download to your iPhone. The store is packed with all kinds of different genres, both fiction to nonfiction. You can access the iBookstore by going to the iBooks app and choosing Store in the top right-hand corner. Ensure you are connected to the internet and the iBookstore will bring up the home page which shows a selection of books on sale as well as any promotional offers.

You can search the store using the search facility at the bottom of the screen or you can select the categories tab which can be found at the top to narrow down your search. You can also see the top charts, top authors and any books you have purchased. If you have another iOS device and you buy a book from the

iBookstore on it, you can have the book download to your iPhone at no extra cost. You can see these in the 'Not on this iPhone' section of the Purchased tab.

Sample/buy a book

To buy a book, search for the one you want and then tap it. An information page will appear showing you the book description, ratings and reviews and any related books. Standard book information is also shown.

As well as being able to share the information via Mail, Twitter and Facebook and even copy the link, you have two choices. You can sample the book or buy it. Tapping Sample downloads a small section of the book to your iPhone for you to read. Tapping the price will prompt you for your Apple ID and this will then download the whole book to your iPhone.

Navigate an ebook

When you are in your iBooks Library, simply tap on a book you want to read and it will open. By flicking your fingers left and right you are able to go back and forth between the pages. You will also see series of dots at the bottom of the screen. This lets you jump directly to a page, the number of which will be displayed below.

At the top of the screen, you will see more options. These include the ability to go back to your Library or select one of the book's chapters. You can adjust the text size and search for certain words and phrases but, handily, using the right-most icon, you can bookmark pages too. Users can even use the highlighter tool to mark important pieces of text.

You can change the brightness by dragging the on-screen slider to the left or to the right

Activate Night mode

1 Find a book Open a book you want to read at night and tap the font option.

2 Select Theme Select the Theme option on the box underneath the font button.

3 Select Night Tap on the word Night and you will notice that the screen goes dark.

4 White on Black The effect is white text on black. You can revert back by tapping Normal.

Read attachments from Mail

When you receive an email with a PDF or ePub attachment, it's possible to send it to iBooks for storage and to read. Simply tap on the PDF and it will open up for you to read. Tap on the Share button in the top right-hand corner, however, and you will be presented with more options for what to do with the file. As well as being able to send it via Mail or print it, you will also be able to Open your PDF in iBooks. Tap on this option and the iBooks app will activate automatically.

Your PDF or ePub file will then be displayed in iBooks and become part of your iBooks library. This allows you to search through it, send it by email and print, produce notes and keep it safe for future reference.

Fig 3 You can save and view PDFs and ePub attachments in iBooks

Library
At the top of the screen, you can go back to your library or, if you have a sample, buy the whole book to read

The book
The book appears in the main part of the screen. As you can see, it looks like a real page of a book with familiar formatting

Themes
Normal is what you see here, Sepia adds a classic hue, and Night features white text on a black background

Options bar
You can also change the font, search and bookmark. Night vision and full page modes are available too

To remove a highlight, select the word or phrase and use the red line icon to delete

To find PDFs in iBooks, tap on the Collections button at the top of the screen and select PDFs. A list of PDFs on your iPhone will show together with a thumbnail of the file.

Annotate and make notes

You can annotate and make notes on an iBook. This is great if you are reading a textbook or educational paper, for instance, as you will be able to highlight certain parts of it and make references which will undoubtedly be a big help with your work and future revision. But even when you're reading a relaxing novel, whenever you need to have this facility it will be there.

Accessing it is easy and is a case of highlighting a word by pressing on it and then using the blue circles to expand the phrase. A selection of options appears on the screen and you can make your choice. Any notes and annotations you make are automatically saved to the book so that you can keep coming back to it for reference without worrying that they have disappeared.

As well as the ability to annotate and make notes, you can also search the text for identical words or phrases which may help you with further comments.

How to take notes

1 Select Tap, hold and drag on a word or phrase and then make a choice between Highlight and Note.

2 Notes Now use the keyboard to write a comment for a note on your selected passage.

Add a bookmark

1 Find a page When you are on a page you want to bookmark, tap the icon in the top right.

2 Red bookmark A bookmark will mark your page and this will remain when you come back.

3 View bookmarks To see your bookmarks, tap the chapter button and select Bookmarks.

4 Remove bookmark To remove a bookmark, simply tap on the red marker and it will disappear.

Pages

Get creative using Pages and put together some truly complex and visually enticing documents

You'll use it to…

Write countless letters
Create perfectly formatted letters to friends and family in any style you like

Make flyers
Make posters, artistic flyers and other eye-catching documents in a few taps

Use notes
Utilise footnotes, endnotes and take advantage of great word-count features

Share your work
Once you're finished, you can easily share your creations via many different services

Export your documents
Export your documents in various different formats for ultimate compatibility

Use the templates
Create visually impressive work by using one of the included templates

Fig 1 (above) Pages is the ultimate word-processing solution for any iPhone user

Fig 2 (right) Flyers and reports take minutes to create and can be a highly professional-looking addition to a business

A word processor on iPhone

Pages is a fully featured word processor which includes many attributes and full compatibility with popular document formats. Everything you need is built in to a wonderfully clean interface. You can download Pages for £6.99/$9.99 from the App Store.

Create invitations & reports

One feature included in the Pages app that almost no other word processor includes is the ability to create flyers, and to do so with a minimum of fuss. From the moment you open the app you are presented with a selection of templates, but you can also make one from scratch.

To make a flyer or an invitation, tap the + button at the top and select Create Document. Select Blank and a blank page to work on will appear. You can now type your message and hit the paintbrush to change the fonts and colours.

Any images you find in Safari can be saved to your Camera Roll and then pasted into Pages. You can now manipulate them by touch alone which will let you change the size of each image and even change the angle at which they are presented.

Reports are created similarly. You can copy rows and columns directly from the Numbers app or by hitting the + icon and embedding charts and tables directly into your report document. The possibilities are endless.

Learn to work with the Apple-designed templates

The great templates that Apple has included in Pages are designed for you to manipulate however you wish.

Tap the + button on the front screen and then Create Document. Now select one of the templates that fit your project. Once you've chosen a template to use, you can tap any of the text and replace it with your own and even replace any image with one that you would prefer to use. You can also move the images anywhere on the document and the text will automatically re-flow around it.

AirPrint

Apple's AirPrint function is utilised in Pages to let you share any document you create straight away with an AirPrint-enabled printer. All you need to do is tap the spanner at the top of the screen and then select Share and Print.

Now choose Print and then tap the Printer option in the next screen. Your iPhone will now search for a suitable printer and give you the option to print it immediately. No wires, no fuss and the most efficient printing experience imaginable.

All the usual features and options that you get when printing are also available, including the number of copies you would like and the range – whether it be the whole document or just certain pages you would like to print.

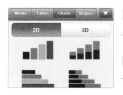

Use the + icon at the top to add in some different media, tables and shapes to your documents

Find and replace

1 Use the spanner Tap the spanner in a document and then select Find from the list.

2 Tap the arrow A box will appear at the top. Tap the arrow to the left of it.

3 Time to type Fill out the Find and Replace boxes with the relevant words and hit Done.

4 Time to replace Now choose Replace or Replace All as required then you're done.

Pages

Working with images

Dealing with images when you're working in Pages is as natural as you could hope for. It almost feels futuristic once you have learned how to manipulate them to your desires.

Any image can be imported into Pages by simply copying it from your Camera Roll or saving it from the web first and then copying and pasting it. You can also tap the + icon when in a document and choose Media to copy any image in your iPhoto photo library to the document. It will be placed full-size in the document and so may look out of place at first, but this is where the magic happens.

Tap on the image in the document and you'll notice the blue dots around it; if you hold and pull any of them you can resize the image by touch alone to see what fits best. Using a finger and

Multiple settings
Many settings are available behind the spanner including document setup and sharing options

Styles
You can choose from multiple fonts and many style options for your text

Inserting media
Photos, tables, charts and shapes can all be inserted into a document with just a couple of taps

Images
Images can be managed in any way you like and moved around the document with ease

Via the settings, you can very easily set up your document header, footer and paper size

thumb you can rotate the image in any way and then move it into the exact position you want by simply sliding it. It really is incredibly easy to work with your images in Pages.

Share your documents

You can share your documents easily in Pages and the process is as simple as everything else you will encounter in this superb app. Tap the spanner icon at the top and then check the various options available to you.

You can email the document and choose which format you want to send it in (PDF, Word or Pages) and then fill in the recipient's email address. The title of the document will form the title of the email so most of the work is already done for you.

You can also copy the document to iTunes for safekeeping or to a WebDAV account by selecting the appropriate option. Remember that if you enabled iCloud when you first ran the app, all of your documents will be automatically stored online for you and are available whenever you need them. There are multiple sharing options and they are all easy to use, so the only thing that you need to do is decide which one to take advantage of.

Open a Pages document in another app

1 Get sharing With your document open, tap the spanner icon and then hit Share and Print.

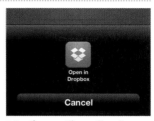

2 Another app Choose Open in Another App, your preferred format and then the app you want.

Export to .doc

1 Find the document Go to the main document screen then tap and hold the document.

2 Open Doc Select and open the document you want, Share then Open In Another App.

3 Time to convert Choose Word from the next screen and the document will start converting.

4 It's exported The file will now be saved in .doc format ready for you to share.

Numbers

Numbers is Apple's answer to Microsoft Excel and you'll find that it succeeds in all the important areas

You'll use it to…

Use clever templates
Build spreadsheets for multiple tasks using the useful built-in templates

Add complex calculations
Take advantage of more than 250 useful functions so Numbers does the thinking

Include your media
Insert photos and videos into all of your spreadsheets to enhance the experience

Share your work
Share your creations with your friends and colleagues in mere seconds

Undo mistakes
You can undo your errors even after a spreadsheet has been closed

Build tables
Build tables and use charts to manage your data and stay on top of your workload

Fig 1 (above) Numbers can handle presenting complex data in a natural way that appeals to everyone

Fig 2 (right) You can create new spreadsheets in Numbers in seconds

Present facts and figures in style

You can present all of your numbers and data in styles that are easily understood by others using Numbers. The prebuilt charts and tables make organising information as easy as can be within a spreadsheet. It's downloadable from the App Store for £6.99/$9.99.

Create a spreadsheet

The process for creating a new spreadsheet in Numbers could not be simpler. However, there are a few choices open to you when you are getting started.

The front screen will show a Getting Started spreadsheet and a + button at the top. Tap the + and you will be presented with the option to create a spreadsheet. Choose this and a selection of templates will appear on screen. If you choose the blank template you will be given a completely blank canvas to work with, but think about the task you want to complete before choosing this and have a look at the templates that are available, just in case a different one will be more suitable. Whatever template you decide upon, simply tap a thumbnailed spreadsheet

and it will fill the screen ready for you to work on. You can now tap on any cell or pinch to make the rows and columns larger and interact with every single part of the new spreadsheet. You'll soon come to realise that creating a new spreadsheet in Numbers is incredibly efficient.

Make a 3D chart

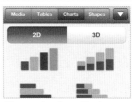

1 Locate the charts Tap the + icon at the top when in a spreadsheet and select Charts.

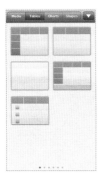

Intelligent tables
The tables built into Numbers are incredibly useful when building new spreadsheets. Tap the + icon at the top when in a spreadsheet and then choose Tables from the top bar.

You will now be able to choose from six screens of tables, each containing five choices in different colours and with specific uses. Some have checkboxes built-in and others are plain and simple which could be useful for presenting simplistic data. Thirty intelligent tables makes Numbers even more useful. There are also a wide range of charts and graphs that can be created from the data. When you select a table it appears below your spreadsheet, so you can manage both aspects of your data at the same time.

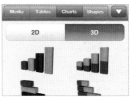

2 Go to 3D Tap 3D and then choose a chart style that you want to use.

Sharing your spreadsheets
When you have finished creating your spreadsheet, sharing it couldn't be simpler. Simply head back to the main screen where all of your files are held and hold your finger down on one of them.

The sharing icon (a curved arrow) will appear at the top and tapping this will bring up options to email the spreadsheet, open it in another app, copy to iTunes or copy to WebDav. You then need to choose the format to share it in and the sharing will be completed. You can share spreadsheets in just four taps which is ideal for fast, seamless file transfers.

3 A simple tap Tap the chart as soon as it's placed in your current spreadsheet.

You can choose as many files as you like to share at once by simply tapping on each one

4 Choose your data Highlight some cells and the data will be added to the chart.

Numbers

Functions and formulas

You have more than 250 functions and formulas at your disposal in Numbers and dealing with so many options is not usually easy on any mobile device. However, the combination of the iPhone screen and clever software implementation make accessing, learning and using them really easy.

To use a specific function, tap any cell and then tap the '=' sign at the top of the keyboard. The keyboard will change and you will see a Functions button at the bottom of the screen. Tap this button and a list of functions will appear which you can select from and immediately add to the cell. If you tap the blue arrow to the right of the function name, you will be able to read a full description of what the function does and how it can be used.

Fig 3 A huge number of functions and formulas are easily accessible when you need them

Media and tables
You can easily insert photos, tables, charts and shapes via this button

Tabs
The tabs can be used to create spreadsheets that contain more than one sheet

Functions
All of the functions you need are perfectly laid out and available

Graphs
Multiple graph styles are available and can be created in seconds using selected data

When you double-tap a cell, note the way the keyboard changes and offers different shortcuts

You can also tap the Categories option at the bottom to access many more useful functions. Formulas are also input through the = sign at which point the keyboard will offer many shortcuts to commonly used functionality. You will need to input instructions manually, but a range of formulas are available to select.

Sliders, steppers and pop-ups

Some functionality within Numbers is designed to speed up data entry and to also ensure that the inputted data is correct.

Sliders are available by selecting a cell, or a range of cells, and then tapping the paintbrush at the top. Choose Format and scroll down to Slider and press the blue arrow. You can now choose the maximum and minimum values and the increments. When you next tap the cell you can adjust the value by simply sliding along the slider that pops up.

Steppers are available in the same screen and once you have input your increments, you can change the values by tapping buttons rather than sliding. Pop-up menus are available from the Format screen too, but are designed to bring up menus when you tap a cell rather than let you input specific data.

Create pop-up menus

1 Find the function Tap the paintbrush when in a cell, select Format and then Pop-up Menu.

2 Add your items Input any text you like and the menu will appear when the cell is double-tapped.

Export to .xls

1 Choose the file Choose a file to export by holding your finger down on it.

2 Time to share Tap the sharing icon at the top and choose your sharing method.

3 Choose Excel Now choose Excel from the options that appear in the next screen.

4 The conversion process The file will now convert to Excel ready for sharing.

Keynote

Keynote

Keynote makes presentation creation easier than ever before and the results are always impressive

You'll use it to…

Use the templates
Create superb presentations using the professionally designed templates

Share your work
Export your work in various different formats for maximum compatibility

Use media
Insert engaging media anywhere in your presentation to bring your work to life

Animate away
Animate aspects of each slide – an ideal way to keep the audience's attention

Control your presentation
Swipe, flick and tap your presentation to control it wirelessly with your iPhone

Keep your work safe
Use iCloud to keep all of your precious work safe, no matter which device you use

Create presentations

Keynote can help you to create sophisticated presentations in mere minutes. You can use the templates or start from scratch, but the end result is almost always exactly what you wish for. Download it from the App Store for £6.99/$9.99.

Make a slideshow

To make your first slideshow using Keynote, open the app on your iPhone and then start by tapping the + icon at the top of the interface. Then select Create Presentation. Browse through the options and choose a simple template such as White or Black and you will be presented with a slide showing an example photo and some text. Double-tap the large text and replace it with your own words and do the same with the smaller text. You can add whatever you like to the first slide and then tap the + icon in the bottom left-hand side of the screen. A new window will pop up and you can select another slide type to insert. Once you have chosen one to

Fig 1 Creating long and complex slideshows feels very natural when you first use Keynote

use, it will fill the main section and be shown as a thumbnail in the left-hand panel. As you add in new slides to your presentation you can hold each thumbnail and drag it to a new position – you can move your slides about in any way you like.

Choosing and managing the individual slides is a very easy process. You'll find that most of your time will be spent writing and adding your content to each one, to make your presentation as exciting as possible.

Flick, tap and drag to navigate your presentation

Holding your finger on a slide thumbnail will select it – you can now drag it to a new position in the slide timeline to change the order in which the slides appear.

Tapping an individual slide will display it in full on the right-hand side for editing and this will help you to decide exactly where in the presentation each slide should be placed. If you have many slides, simply flick up and down the thumbnails to see slides that are off the screen.

Share your presentation

After you're finished creating, sharing a presentation takes only a few seconds. When in a presentation, tap the spanner at the top and then choose Share and Print. You can now choose to email it or open it in another app. You can also copy it to iTunes or to WebDAV for safe keeping, but there are more than enough options for most people to share their work in any way they like. When exporting, an option will pop up to choose which exact format the presentation should be shared in.

You can delete individual slides by holding your finger down and using the pop-up menu

Add animations

1 Use the spanner Tap the spanner at the top and select Transitions and Builds.

2 Useful pop-ups A self-explanatory pop-up will appear. Dismiss it.

3 Obvious indicators Tap a slide and the tap the pop-up icon next to it.

4 Choose your animation Now select the type of animation you want and the timing.

GarageBand

GarageBand

GarageBand is a recording studio in your pocket with the ability to recreate instruments perfectly

You'll use it to…

Remember new tunes
If you suddenly think of a new tune or chord you can capture it immediately

Play new instruments
Play any instrument from a vast number of offerings for a symphony of sounds

Use your own equipment
Attach your own instruments and then play and record them instantly

Keep in sync
A great way to manage all of your songs automatically using the iCloud

Mix and match
Mix many instruments and sounds into one multilayered song for amazing results

Jam with friends
Play along with friends using wireless connections and make music together

Music made easy

GarageBand is capable of acting as a mini recording studio for all of your instruments. You can play many of the included instruments on the app or simply plug your own in for added realism. It's downloadable from the App Store for £2.99/$4.99.

Create a song

Creating a song in GarageBand is as simple as doing so with real musical instruments. The interface is obvious enough to let anyone jump in and start straight away.

Begin by choosing an instrument from the many that are available via the Instruments icon in the drop down menu in the top right of the screen. Once you have decided what you want to make music with, tap the red Record button at the top and start playing. You will hear a metronome in the background to help you keep time, and as soon as you are satisfied with what you've done, press Stop at the top.

Fig 1 You can layer several instrument tracks together to create a musical masterpiece

You can now play your track back to hear what it sounds like. It will be saved automatically, so you needn't worry about losing any of your musical masterpieces.

Keyboards

Within the instruments section you will see an option called Keyboard. Tap this and a keyboard will immediately fill up the screen. Go back to the drop down menu, tap Grand Piano and you will see the selected keyboard highlighted in the window that pops up. You will now see a selection of keyboards shown on the screen and a row of choices just above them. Each choice at the top includes eight instruments, making a total of 48. Experimenting with each will help you realise which one you need. Just tap a picture of a keyboard and it will fill the screen straight away with a realistic design so you know for sure which one you are using.

Drums

Within the instruments selector there are eight different drum kits to choose from. Enter the Instruments panel and select Drums to see all of the choices which range from Classic Studio Kit to a Hip Hop Drum machine. Each type of kit will produce very different sounds and so you may want to experiment with each of them before you start recording.

You can also tap the Settings cog icon in the top right-hand corner to adjust the echo, reverb and all sorts of other options that can change the tone of your finished creation. On some kits you can also play around with the resonance and cutoff via the circular volume buttons at the top. Be sure to also check out the Smart Drums to get a helping hand with your beat creation.

Choose Sampler from instruments to record a sound that will be played by the keyboard

Export your song

1 Find your songs Tap the My Songs icon, found on the left of the top bar.

2 Select a song Hold your finger on a song thumbnail and then select the Share icon above it.

3 Sharing options A list will appear showing all of the ways you can share the song.

4 Time to export When you choose an option, the song will export as required.

iMovie

Let your imagination run wild with iMovie and make professional, fun and unique creations every time

Create & edit films

iMovie is designed to let you simply drop media including videos and photos into it and to then edit them all together. The end result is a movie format that looks as though you spent hours creating a masterpiece. In reality, you can create that masterpiece in minutes. It's downloadable from the App Store for £2.99/$4.99.

Make a movie with trailers

You may wonder how trailers can work within videos, but in iMovie the idea has been taken to a whole new level. To use a trailer, tap the + button in the centre of the screen and choose New Trailer from the pop-up. You will now be presented with a selection of trailers in a horizontal form that you can preview. Tap the play button on each trailer and it will start playing so that you can be sure the theme fits with the content or event you are building the movie for. When you have found one, tap the Create icon at the top-right and a new screen will pop up for you to personalise.

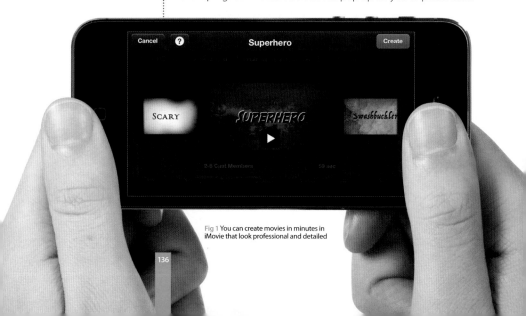

Fig 1 You can create movies in minutes in iMovie that look professional and detailed

You can type in the name of the movie, the cast members and even credits to show at the end. You can then create a storyboard by tapping the relevant icon and when you add media it will be annotated with the topics you have input. Trailers are easy, effective and stunning to watch.

Add titles and transitions

You can add titles to any image in iMovie by selecting an image from the Camera Roll and then double-tapping it at the bottom. Now choose your title style and then type in the words in the text box that appears.

Transitions between images and videos are handled by double-tapping the small arrows between the objects and then using the scroll wheel to choose the one you want to use. It all works by using simple touches.

Film from within the app

iMovie works perfectly with media you have already captured, but you can take new photos and videos while you are in the app and add them to a new project straight away.

In the editing screen, look for the camcorder icon which is placed to the right in the centre line. Tap it and you will be taken to the normal camera screen. Notice at the bottom that you can select between film and photo. Simply make your choice and snap the media to add into your movie. Then tap Use to include it in your project immediately. This is perfect for when you want to grab a few incidental shots to help piece your project together and make the whole thing run a bit smoother.

You can select transitions that range from 0.5 seconds to two seconds. Try to use the shorter ones for consistency

Import footage

1 Tap the button Tap the media button on the left-hand side of the screen.

2 The media screen Select the type of media you want using the buttons at the bottom.

3 Choose an item Tap a photo or video and it will jump into your current project.

4 Import the media You can now manipulate the imported footage to your preference.

iMovie

Fig 2 Trailers bring lots of fun and plenty of special effects to all of your movies

Fig 3 Themes can add a great touch of personality to all of your movie creations

Use iMovie themes

Themes in iMovie are much more subtle than trailers. Themes are intended to give you an environment for your movie to play within, rather than offer special effects that build around a storyline.

From the editing screen, tap the cog icon which is in the top right-hand corner and you will be presented with a selection of thumbnails which designate each theme available to you. Once you have chosen one that you want to use, highlight it then press Done. It will then be added to your project. You will now need to play the movie to see what it looks like and if you are not happy, simply press the cog again and select another one. This is by far the best way to test each theme until you find the one you prefer.

You can also choose to use the music that is embedded in the theme, or select some music to add in from your own music library

Precise manipulation
Every single clip can be manipulated precisely using the yellow handles and displayed information

So many themes
You can choose from a selection of themes via this button and also use it to manipulate many other settings

Transitions
You can add transitions between elements and even title each photo within the movie

Visually aware
At any time you can zoom in to see exactly how your finished movie will look

To make some precision edits, you can pinch to zoom in to each clip and examine it up close

stored on your smartphone. You will also be able to set a default fade from black or white for the entire theme in the settings screen if you wish.

The Precision Editor

The Precision Editor is extremely effective for creating professional-looking clips and it gives you a lot of control over each part of your movie, but it is not obvious how it should be used at first. The process is, however, very natural and quite easy to use once you understand the basics. It's worth taking some time to get used to it and the results will make the effort worthwhile.

All you need to do is tap on a photo or video in your timeline and then look for the yellow bars with circles at the top of them. Think of these as handles that you can drag into position, because this is exactly what they are. As you move them along, you will see detailed information in the top half of the screen that lets you precisely choose how long each clip should be and where it should start and end. Play around with these precision controls to see exactly what you can achieve with this feature, and when you're happy, watch your movie back!

Accurate positioning

1 **Grab the handle** Tap and hold a yellow circle and move it. Notice the timer at the top.

2 **Back to the start** You can also tap the icon to jump straight to the start of the clip.

Export to Camera Roll

1 **Find your movie** Press the top-left icon to be taken back to the main movie screen.

2 **Time to send** Press the sharing icon at the bottom and then choose Camera Roll.

3 **Choose your size** Now choose the quality of the movie you want to export.

4 **Export completed** The movie may take time to export, but it will complete eventually.

iPhoto

iPhoto

iPhoto is the only photo-editing tool you will need because the feature set is so versatile

You'll use it to…

Edit your photos
Add effects to your photos and fix problems

Create journals
Build journals of special events in minutes

Share your work
Stream or share photos on social networks

Manage your collection
Pick out your best shots with touch gestures

Paint away
Paint colours and fixes over existing images

Compare your snaps
Compare photos side by side to choose

Edit and organise your photo collection

With iPhoto you can organise hundreds of photos using lots of different criteria and also compare selections to help you decide which ones to keep that look similar. It is a dream solution for anyone with a camera!

Smart browsing

Managing a photo collection that contains hundreds of photos is not easy and finding individual snaps is even more difficult. iPhoto, however, now brings all of the searching power of its desktop equivalent to the iPhone which lets you search and find what you need in many different ways in seconds.

When you open iPhoto you will see a strip at the bottom with four icons included. You will need to sync your iPhone with iTunes to ensure that you can use all of these, but once done you will be able to browse through your photo collection by album, individual photo, events and journals. This means that if you need to find a snap taken at a particular time or in one place you can find it relatively easily. The clever split-screen view helps when you open one

Fig 1 Managing and editing your photo collection is much easier with iPhoto

of the categories and lets you tap individual thumbnails and see them full-screen, even while all of the other thumbnails are on display. It all works efficiently and accurately. This means that you can quickly locate similar photos by having one full screen while you scroll through the thumbnail list at the bottom of the screen to find others.

Multi-touch editing

It is likely that many of your photos will require some form of adjustment and this is another area that iPhoto shines in.

Select any photo and tap the Edit icon at the top to start the process. You can now use your fingers to pinch and zoom to see the full detail or to edit specific parts of each photograph via the icons found at the bottom of the screen. You can manipulate the sky, grass and any other aspect of each photo by touch alone. The icons at the bottom of the screen allow you to make all manner of changes, so be sure to use the information icon to find out about how they each can help.

The Swatch Book

One feature that is not noticeable at first is the Swatch Book. This is a handy element of iPhoto that contains a host of effects, all of which can be applied and removed with just one simple tap.

Find the effects icon at the bottom of the screen, it looks like a collection of stars, and tap it. A series of swatches will magically appear and include artistic, vintage and black-and-white tones. Choose one and you will see it settle at the bottom of the screen. Slide your finger along the swatch and the tones will change in gradients. It's a true highlight of the entire iPhoto experience.

Some tweaks are hidden behind icons, so tap the help icon to see what they do

Resize and crop

1 Find the icon Locate the crop icon in the bottom-left corner and tap it.

2 Create squares Hold your finger on the screen to bring up the crop grid.

3 Pinch to zoom You can now pinch with your fingers to change the size of the photo.

4 Choose any section It is easy to select any part of a photo to fill the frame.

141

iPhoto

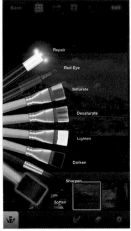

Fig 2 The brushes let you change and improve every single part of a photo

Brushes

Perhaps the most artistic feature in iPhoto is the brush selection which can be used to spruce up and correct or hide flaws in any image. Apple has implemented brushes in such a way that it really is up to you how you use them and the built-in flexibility is huge.

When you tap the brushes icon at the bottom of the screen a selection will pop up for you to choose from. There are eight different choices and when you select one, you then use your finger to add that particular effect to a part of the photo.

The first choice is Repair which can be used to remove areas of the photo and this is useful if something just isn't quite right – zoom in as far as possible when using this and you can be very precise in what you remove. You can lighten specific areas, remove the

The output
You can share your photos or build journals from them, all via this small icon

Ultimate customisation
You can manually tweak every single aspect of each photo for the ultimate in customisation

Comparisons
Selecting multiple photos lets you compare them to choose the best one

Automation
Many tools in iPhoto let you automatically enhance all or parts of your photos

You can undo any changes you make with a brush by tapping the Revert icon at the top

red-eye effect and soften and sharpen to your heart's content. No matter what you want to do to your photos, the brushes feature offers everything you need.

Photo Journals

The Photo Journal feature is a clever way to show your events and pictorial history to others in a pleasing and professional way. You can play around a lot with this feature and once you have created a new journal and chosen the photos to use in it, you can then move the photos around, resize them in any way you like and add titles and other aspects to bring some life to the presentation.

As an easy way to create a slide show of a holiday and to highlight the most important moments, the photo journal's features are guaranteed to work for everyone, no matter how much experience they have of photo curation.

You may also find that the journals you create will be what you look at the most in the future because of their ability to tell a story in one page much more effectively than simply browsing through a selection of photos. Creating a Photo Journal is an amazing way to preserve your most precious memories.

Create a new journal

1 **Choose an event** Tap the sharing button at the top and choose the Journal option.

2 **The content** Select the photos that you want to use and tap Create Journal. That's it – you're done!

Share on social media

1 **Share an image** View a photo, and tap the sharing icon to be offered multiple social options.

2 **What to share** Choose a network and then select the exact photo you want to share.

3 **Time to send** The photo will be prepared and you can then add a brief description.

4 **Share multiple photos** You can share many photos at once to Facebook which saves time.

Enjoyed this book?

Exclusive offer for new

Try
3 issues
for just
£5*

* This offer entitles new UK direct debit subscribers to receive their first three issues for £5. After these issues, subscribers will then pay £25.20 every six issues. Subscribers can cancel this subscription at any time. New subscriptions will start from the next available issue. Offer code ZGGIPCM must be quoted to receive this special subscriptions price. Direct debit guarantee available on request. This offer will expire 31 July 2014.

** This is a US subscription offer. The USA issue rate is based on an annual subscription price of £65 for 13 issues, which is equivalent to approx $100 at the time of writing compared with the newsstand price of $15.50 for 13 issues, being $201.50. Your subscription will start from the next available issue. This offer expires 31 July 2014.

Written by Apple users **for Apple users**

In-depth tutorials
Over 50 pages of tutorials for every major Apple device and application including iPhone, iPad, iPhoto and OS X

The latest news and reviews
All Apple products and accessories tested

iPhone and iPad
An essential resource for all iPhone and iPad users

About the mag

subscribers to...

iCreate™

Try 3 issues for £5 in the UK*
or just $7.69 per issue in the USA**
(saving 50% off the newsstand price)

For amazing offers please visit
www.imaginesubs.co.uk/icr
Quote code ZGGIPCM
Or telephone UK 0844 848 8401 Overseas +44 (0) 1795 592 865

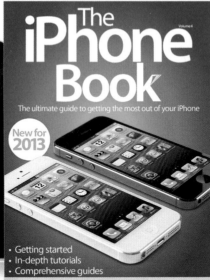